GROUNDRUSH

The first successful
jump at Cheddar Gorge

GROUND-
RUSH

Simon Jakeman

JONATHAN CAPE
LONDON

First published 1992
© Simon Jakeman 1992
Jonathan Cape, 20 Vauxhall Bridge Road, London SW1V 2SA

Simon Jakeman has asserted his right
under the Copyright, Designs and Patents Act, 1988
to be identified as the author of this work

A CIP catalogue record for this book
is available from the British Library

ISBN 0-224-03534-7

Phototypeset by Computape (Pickering) Ltd, North Yorkshire
Printed in Great Britain by
Mackays of Chatham PLC, Chatham, Kent

Contents

Illustrations

My thanks must go to a number of people without whose help and hard work this would still be an untidy pile of handwritten notes on a shelf. To protect their privacy I will refer to my close friends by only their first names but my appreciation of Ros, Karina, Antoinette, Jackie, Ralph, Nick D.G., Michele and Jana is no less for that. For permission to use their photographs I acknowledge Steve F., Chris L., Ginge, Pat and Jana. The photograph of skydiving over Houston, Texas, was kindly supplied by Jean Boenish and the jacket photograph by Richie Stein. Finally I must thank also Leo Dickinson for leading me to a publisher and my editor, Tony Colwell, for his unflagging support.

S.J.
February 1992

Foreword

This true story is about the relationship of risk to fear, and the misunderstanding with which it is sometimes seen. Some readers may dispute points of technicality: scholars of physics may quote formulae when it comes to mass, acceleration, distance, timing and the like. If there is a discrepancy it can be only a few feet here or a fraction of a second there, and I have done my best to make it accurate.

Many of these adventures, while not illegal, are not totally above board, and so some names have been altered to give my friends a measure of protection. But, in any case, the play is done, and to chastise us so long after the event would be an empty gesture.

In order to thread together the underlying theme I have manifested the 'carrion man', or 'harpie'. In Greek mythology a harpie is a malevolent spirit of the air, a kind

9

of Medusa with wings and claws. The carrion man is one who feasts upon the dead and the dying, a ghoul. Two names for one spectre which has many guises. They are around, though not always so monstrous as I have described them.

I have tried to show the reasoning of those who are attracted by and who would romance this 'carrion man'. Classically, when the adventurer looks at the gorgon he is rooted to the spot and turned into a pillar of salt. That is the taste of tears, and this is how it begins.

> . . . *And if the calling comes to you as black leather wings beat in the darkness outside, will you dare to slip the catch and look into the face of the carrion man . . . ?*

GROUNDRUSH

From the high tors,
   Where the old gods sleep.
In the golden meadows.
From the crystal streams in secret woods,
    I have sought for you.

I

The Incubation

Ten years roughnecking in the construction business teaches you a lot. Kids arrive fresh out of school, green and gullible, but within a few weeks they become educated so that by their first winter they are as wise as the next man. You grow up or you go under. It's an efficient process and good street education, but it should really be seen as simply a means of survival.

For me, ten years' renovation work in London's East End meant ten hot summers swinging sledgehammers, ripping out ceilings or running up and down ladders all day with bricks and cement. Or it meant eight hours a day spent knee-deep in water in a hole in the ground, constantly bent over, digging the heavy clay from between timber struts braced so that a few tons of dirt didn't decide to bury me down there. Some days there would have been nothing more I could have wished for.

Winters were the worst. In one old house where we went to start work we found the stiffened corpse of a tramp who had died from the cold. There was a foul smell as we unboarded the door, and in a back room we found him frozen to death. He was slumped against a wall with beer cans strewn around and newspapers for lighting a fire stacked beside him. At another site there was a group of alcoholics living in the derelict property next door. We returned from our Christmas break to find the police investigating the remains of somebody who'd been hacked to death with one of our pick-axes. A festive drinking session which had got a little out of hand. On the colder mornings we sat huddled together in the back of the van, hoping that the heavy traffic would prevent us from reaching our destination for a few precious minutes more.

Of course there were good times too, warm days when you arrived wearing just your shorts, and by the end of May were already the colour of tobacco. I remember working on a rooftop in the city, ripping out the rotted timber and reslating alongside a ten-storey office block, all tinted glass, gorgeous women and air conditioning. On site, we pitied the office workers and revelled in our freedom. Tiptoeing along the ridges three or four floors up, we'd perform for our audience and laugh at their caged existence. But the wheel would soon turn and along would come winter again, when they would laugh right back at us.

Because of its clangorous, sprawling street-theatre air, the building trade is a breeding ground for flamboyant characters. Some of these people have worked with hardened hands and aching backs for up to fifty years. Most of them have never spent a working day indoors, and though everyone complains, few would change. It is a merciless playground where weakness soon results in social predation. You have to learn the code of a rough friendliness while all the time maintaining a self suffi- ciency. You have to be as sharp as everyone else and you must always be able to pull your weight. As my old friend Sharkey would say, 'If you're gonna run with the big dogs you gotta learn to piss high.'

And when the pack turns, you'd better be ready to turn with it, though that doesn't mean you have to be in at the kill. Usually it's the same wolves letting the blood every time. The pack code brings out the natural bully, though mostly in a good-natured and instructive way. So if some hyena is stupid enough to get his arse bitten, you'd do best to let him fight his own battle. We once had a 'social conscience' start work on one of our sites; a gent who began preaching in the lunch break about our rights. He tried to tell a hutful of semi-literate, no-fixed-abode, cash-in-hand, dole-drawing Irish labourers why they should join a union. No one liked the idea. If a man works, he gets paid, and if he doesn't come in one morning no one's going to ask why. In your wage packet, a day spent drunk is a day short. The gent lasted little more than a week. Someone in the bosses' shed must have heard the word union, for they soon sacked him. He couldn't piss very high.

Unlike our carpenter, Harry the Hat. Harry had a ragged scar down his back where a docker's hook had been stuck through him in a fight in the Gulf of Aqaba. Drawing on his travels with the merchant navy, Harry was a great story teller. Being young and curious myself, and always ready to benefit from other people's experiences, I once asked Harry what he had learned in his sixty years of adventuring. After thinking about it for a long time he gave me his answer: life, he said, was about taking everything that's on offer; to live each day as fiercely as you can. As an afterthought he added something I've many times since found to be true. 'Be sure of one thing,' Harry said: 'you can never tell what's going to happen next.'

As if to prove his point, Harry died from a brain haemorrhage just one week after passing on his lifetime's wisdom. It was a cruel twist – and spooky if I thought about it too much. That was ten years ago now, and Harry remains dead, but then death lasts for a long time.

A construction site is a dangerous place where bravado is the order of the day. But it's a stage for comedy too, and the best comedians I knew were Big Dave and the Weasel. As drainage king, Dave could get a fall on a pipe where it was all but impossible, so that the soil looked as if it was flowing uphill from the outlet to the manhole. He could tell exactly what was blocking a four-inch drain by probing into the dark water with ten sections of screw-together rod. There was a joke around at that time about a gynaecologist who'd decorated his house through the letter box. Dave had the same kind of hands.

The underworld, though, really belonged to the forty-five-year-old schoolboy called Weasel – a tiny, wiry figure who always wore a grey suit to work. A wrinkled mud-spattered suit for sure, but a suit none the less. Weasel could get down the tiniest manhole, and the deepest. This was certainly impressive – because while the suit never looked any the worse, the Weasel suffered from chronic claustrophobia. When once, for a joke, Dave had replaced the cast iron cover over the manhole down which the Weasel had vanished, there was a pregnant pause before our rodent friend suffered a fit of terror (due either to his imprisonment or to his fear of approaching unpleasantness) and Big Dave, the iron cover, and the added weight of Dave's considerable lunchtime Guinness intake, were lifted with desperately inspired strength lightly to one side.

A lot of the time you work in gangs, and the bosses set one gang against another, each tearing down and gutting the inside of a house. Each gang is split into pairs, with a gangerman presiding. I was once offered the post of gangerman but I declined it. Anyone promoted to ganger gets the power of 'the shout' and is alienated from the other men, but it's the camaraderie that keeps you sane, and I valued my sanity more than the few pounds extra pay.

In the summer of eighty-four, I was working with an American named Jeff Smith who came from a small town in West Virginia. His father was in the United States Air Force, and so Jeff had travelled the world before ending up swinging a sledgehammer next to me in the East End of London. We used to take our lunch up on the roof, though that summer the tar was usually too hot to sit on by eight in the morning. From four floors up you could see right across London, the jumble of houses just fading away into the distant haze. In the centre of town the buildings towered four, five and six hundred feet into the sky, like so many grey megaliths. One day, while we were gazing out, Jeff nodded towards the taller towers and asked casually, 'Anybody ever jump off one of them?'

'Must have,' I replied. 'Living off stocks and shares would make any man feel suicidal at times.'

'No, man!' Jeff said, laughing. 'I mean parachute jump.'

'If they did, then I've never heard of it.'

The nearer towers were those of the Barbican, three great black thirty-nine-storey blocks with balconies jutting out four hundred feet above the road.

'Too low,' I said. 'And nowhere to land even if you did.'

A storm was brewing to the south and the air began to get so heavy that you felt you could cut it. It had been growing hazier all day and I'd developed a bad headache. Midges began weaving excitedly. When the air pressure slumped, Jeff and I were sent up to sheet over the open roof beams. The wind picked up while we worked, a sure sign that the storm was imminent. Handling a twenty-foot-square tarpaulin blowing in all directions while we balanced forty feet up on a parapet wall, with a hammer in one hand and a bunch of nails clenched between our teeth, was not an easy way to make a living. We were glad to have the job finished as the first heavy drops clattered across the sheet.

Inside our top floor tent we stood looking out. The sky had grown black with thunderclouds that were being squeezed out right over us. Then came the first of the lightning – no forked crack in the sky, just an indistinct flash followed seconds later by a low rumble.

'Man, back home,' Jeff said, 'if you see a cloud you take a picture of it and hang it on your wall.'

'Yeah? You know, one day I'm gonna get away to someplace warm like that,' I said.

'I'm going back next year. Just need a little more cash and I'm in the wind.'

We stood in silence and watched the rain teem down.

*

To this day I do not know what strange compulsion made me quit my job and embark on the journey. A yearning had stirred inside me, and though I knew not what lay ahead, to stay became unthinkable. It was as if the nature of the trap – that of inconsequence – had come suddenly into perspective. Threatened with asphyxiation, escape became my only thought. I was seized by a wild desire to get out of the machine. One minute I was painting timber under a clear blue sky and the next an aeroplane came buzzing overhead, very low, so that you could see the door. I threw the paintbrush across the yard, walked into the foreman's office and told him to make up my papers. With no plan and only a small amount of cash I found myself that night heading west.

Work is a necessary burden which few really enjoy and generally it is a means to an end. For some people their work is their passion; most of us just need the money. In almost every case where passion finds us, however subtle the attraction, it holds us mercilessly to ransom. It may be a dream home and the ensuing mortgage, gambling, skiing or the love of travel, but whatever form it takes it must be paid for. These lovers we take are heartless and will lie with any who can afford them.

My passion was for skydiving and I could not stand the thought of being without it. Jeff knew that during any time out over the last few years I had spent every penny I could muster, sweating or freezing next to him, on one-way tickets to twelve thousand feet. Every weekend I would drive out into the countryside and pay for the pleasure of plunging two miles straight down, alone or in a group, at a tiny Devonshire airfield.

Out of the bustling city and through the flat uniform suburbs I went. Tower blocks appeared less often and the houses were cleaner and newer, unlike their crumbling inner-city counterparts. I watched the west-bound motorways become choked with vehicles as motorists jockeyed for position in the barely moving gridlock. When engineers design roads they work to guidelines of speed, space and volume of traffic, but if these last two categories don't balance then a speed debt occurs and each car must slow down or stop in order to pay it. When I arrived in the west country I was still running at big-city speed and found that a considerable gearing down was necessary. Surrendering the controls to fate I drifted into the slow lane, blissfully unaware of the fortune that was thundering toward me.

That summer the air in Devon was so still that you could hear the windrush of bodies falling two miles above your head. Once, flying at eleven thousand feet, we could see the Bristol Channel on one side of the aircraft and far away across the checkerboard farmland below the English Channel on the other. Soon I had got myself into a parachute display team and this paid good money. From two displays a week, instruction jumps with student parachutists, washing aeroplanes and packing other people's chutes, I found that it was possible to earn enough to survive from day to day quite comfortably if a little precariously.

It was one of those golden summers that seem to last for

ever with one cloudless hot day after another. We would make the day's last jump at sunset, falling in a group through ragged orange skies, flashing colour and light high in the hazy summer air − air that was so crisp and clean compared to the smoke of London. Every scent from the hedgerows, every sound drifting across the meadows was a treasure; I couldn't have been happier. I wanted for nothing and was fulfilled by each day's passing. Sometimes the jump centre would close for the day and usually I would take the opportunity to hitch a ride the five miles into town. Half-way down the winding lane that led to the airfield, an old stone bridge crossed the river, with a lush meadow beside it. Often in the late afternoon I would have nothing better to do than sit on the wooden fence and talk to the cows that would gather round me, all huge rolling eyes and wet noses.

The feeling of having escaped was a hedonistic thrill and I wore its prize of irresponsibility for all to see, though, of course, there is both a positive and negative side to every situation. The lack of security was not so bad in reality as it was in prospect, but it was there. If I got cold turkey for the creature comforts of the city, the pleasures of the gypsy life soon made up for the bland fruits of my former hated labours.

*

Life on the road had an irresistible romance to it. We would skydive into an agricultural show in one of the villages, not knowing until we arrived overhead what the place looked like or how big the landing zone was. Then, after a brief freefall, we would open our chutes and float down into the arena to the sound of the village band playing and people clapping, while the announcer spurred them on with the grandest of fairground banter.

While we repacked on the edge of the field people would ask us questions about our strange occupation, their children waving programmes for us to sign. The questions were always the same, you could put money on that. How fast do you fall? Can you breathe? And the amazingly sincere, 'What do you do if your chutes don't open?'

'Well, we each have a reserve.'

'But what if that doesn't open?'

'Well, we'd die of course.'

And they would shake their heads in astonishment.

One of my jump partners on this team was Eddie Norris, and we would always sign our autographs as Captain Jaques and Eddie of the Skies. We perpetuated the myth of the flying circus sky gypsies with merciless self-indulgence. The children's parents would feel the fabric of our parachutes and nod wisely, lighted cigarettes inches from causing irreparable damage. Then they would turn, thanking us for the show, and walk over the rigging lines as they hurried back to see the motorcycle display team defy death once more, or to throw wet sponges at the vicar to help pay for his new church roof.

As soon as we had secured our chutes in the team bus, a battered blue transit van with various panels taped or tied on, we would find the beer tent. Free beer and burgers and endless skydiving tales told to small-town country girls. The village boys hated us, but we did not care. We would skydive in, drink and tell tall stories, ravish as many of their women as we could, and then leave in a cloud of dust and drunken promises.

I remember jumping into one place at sunset when there was thick cloud at three thousand feet. The sun was below the uniform grey blanket as we flew in a mile overhead and saw the drop zone through a perfect round break in the clouds. It was like diving into a volcano, with the red glow to be seen through the hole and the darkness in the sky above. In freefall, lying on my stomach on a mattress of loud rushing air, I peered through the hole at the fields below, and when I opened my parachute inside the cloud walls of the volcano, I could hear a rock band performing outdoors, playing us down with 'Born to Be Wild'.

During this period I became adept at handling the equipment. Through packing innumerable students' parachutes I learned to untangle the lines in seconds. Imagine the amount of entanglement possible with twenty-four rigging lines, any one of which can be used more than once. Student parachutists, who have learned how to land safely rather than how to pack, usually get most of these combinations firmly tied as soon as they touch down. I often wondered if students purposely landed several miles from the airfield, and always at dusk, in order to get the last few tangles into place before the irate instructor found them.

A parachute is basically a simple device and, if packed anywhere near properly, it will open. I have known people who lovingly smooth and iron out every fold during packing and others who throw the canopy into the container and pull it on to their backs. Sometimes you may be in a hurry and pack a little untidily, so you sit in the plane on the climb to your exit altitude and think, wow – this opening will be interesting. You might even tell the jumper next to you to watch you open so that he can see how bad it is. But it always opens.

On the rare and spectacular occasion when one's chute does malfunction it is a surprise which demands immediate action. Every jumper will be in that situation at some time or other, and those who don't believe it are deluding themselves. In eleven hundred jumps I have had to open my reserve chute four times, and each time I had packed my main canopy as usual. Malfunction strikes like a bolt from the blue. You pull the ripcord for the fifth time that day and everyone else stops falling. Suddenly you find that you are ten seconds from impact and still travelling earthward at a hundred and twenty miles an hour. You'd better do something, quick! Don't bother about feeling scared, just do something. *Now*!

Usually malfunctions are other people's misfortune. Because they are so rare, the odds on it being your turn are small. Everyone carries a reserve, but they are forgotten about until needed. My brother once said that his reserve was the most putrid shade of yellow that he had ever seen, and someone wisely pointed out that if ever he had to use it, it would look beautiful to him.

2

The Key and the Coin

On days when bad weather kept us grounded we would sit in the warmth of the airfield canteen. Outside the misted windows gulls glided along the ranks of tied-down aircraft, mocking at skydivers and pilots alike. The dayglo orange wind socks tugged at their moorings and the low clouds spat rain across the runways.

It was one stormy afternoon on the eve of August when a friend of mine, Steve Mullins, introduced me to Terry who lived in Bristol and divided his free time between rock-climbing and jumping. Climbers in that area have many venues in which to pursue their pleasure, from the long stretches of black rock that tower above the river at Avon Gorge to the crags and precipices of South Wales just across the Sevèrn Bridge. I hadn't reckoned on it as a fateful meeting and so was unaware that, in the midst of our conversation, a key was passed to us. In from the storm an unseen visitor had entered and, moving among the crowd, she had come to stand at our table. She pressed her cold lips to each of us in turn while passing the key, and as an intoxicated man falls into sleep, we three surrendered.

'Take a look at this,' Steve said, gesturing to Terry who produced from his coat pocket a small booklet. I read the title and thumbed through a few of the pages. It was a climbers' manual for the Cheddar Gorge area just south of Bristol.

'Sorry guys,' I said, 'I'm really not into the Spiderman trip. Rock-climbing scares the hell out of me.'

They laughed, and Steve said, 'Yeah, me too. But that's not it. Look at page sixteen.'

It's a strange fact that a lot of skydivers confess to being scared of heights. When falling through the air thousands of feet above the ground, there is nothing around you and the illusion of flight is very convincing. High places, on the other hand, remind one of danger and fear. Page sixteen showed a diagram, a dotted line weaving across several pitches of a cliff face called High Rock.

'No way,' I said. The total height of the pitches amounted to three hundred and sixty vertical feet. 'You will not get me up there. Call me dumb but I'm not crazy.'

'We don't want to get *up* it,' said Terry, grinning.

I sipped my coffee while wondering what madness was coming.

'We want to get *down* from it,' explained Steve.

'Ah, down from it,' I repeated slowly.

'Tomorrow morning.' Terry was grinning now, and

his enthusiasm spread to Steve. They regarded me from the other side of the table through the cigarette smoke and steam from the coffee. Slowly my brain made the connection.

'You're going to make a skydive into Cheddar Gorge?'

'He's got it!' Steve exclaimed.

'Early tomorrow morning, about six o'clock. We went to look at it last week. It's a sheer cliff, three hundred and sixty feet from the overhang straight to the ground.' Terry leaned forward as he spoke.

'What's at the bottom?' I asked. 'Other than strait-jackets and plasma.'

'A big, empty car park. Nothing but dust and grass. There are a few rocks and trees around, but plenty of room to land.'

'This storm is meant to break this evening,' Steve said, 'and if the conditions are calm enough at dawn, we're going for it.'

They both sat back in their chairs with the full depth of their madness laid before me.

*

All skydivers know of a fringe discipline called BASE jumping. Depending on your politics, BASE jumpers are cavaliers or cowboys who use their parachutes to jump from fixed objects rather than moving aircraft. The rules of parachuting state that all openings must be made above two thousand feet. This is to ensure that the jumper has enough time to use his reserve chute if need be. Most BASE jumps – like the one proposed to me – are from fixed points far below two thousand feet. A skydiver died some years ago after jumping from a London tower block, and as far as I knew the group was no longer operative.

On the face of it, BASE jumping was a cheap mistress who paid rich dividends, but underlying the physical danger and the elation of success was a hidden threat which none of us saw – the wretched addiction to risk.

We tend to believe that in anything our chances improve with success. They do not. If you flip a coin four hundred and ninety-nine times and it comes down heads every time, the odds of the five hundredth throw being heads are still exactly fifty/fifty.

The first time I jumped from an aeroplane I pushed myself through the experience, as most people do, with blind trust in my equipment, and instructors spoke with a voice no less quiet than my fear. Even when the jumper exiting before me had a malfunction and opened his reserve, I told myself that probability was now in my favour. I recalled friends who had been in the same situation and had returned unharmed, richer for the experience. I thought of young girls on the ground two thousand feet beneath me who were veterans of many jumps. I told myself whatever I needed to hear to get myself out of the aircraft.

At this early stage in one's jumping career the parachute is opened automatically by means of a 'static line'. A thick webbing strap leads from a strongpoint inside the plane to a special cord at the top of your parachute. As you jump out the static line pulls the parachute canopy from your backpack, and when all the rigging lines are paid out, the cord breaks. The static line stays attached to the plane and you are left hanging under your open parachute.

Later comes freefall, during which you open your

parachute manually. A small round pilot chute, stowed in a pouch on your harness, is attached to the main canopy, and as you fall you extract it and throw it into the moving air. This pilot chute pulls out the main canopy. Having learned to control your fear of leaving the air-craft on a static line, you return to square one with your first freefall. Now several years and a few hundred jumps down the road, I felt that familiar sensation once more.

'This is a fine madness,' I said.

Terry agreed. Steve nodded also.

'You're in then?'

I stared at my coffee while the storm hurled rain against the window and the television set droned on. Perhaps tomorrow would be stormy too. Holding the five hun-dredth coin in my hand, I told myself the necessary lies and hurled it high into the air.

'I'm in.'

We spent the rest of the afternoon talking it over. Excitement overcame my doubts. Fired by the attraction of risk, we left for Steve's house and made preparations for our trip to the gorge the following morning.

Steve lived in an ivy-covered cottage set in an enor-mous rambling garden which backed on to a Norman church. The road led into his village and a hundred yards later it led out of the other side, so that if you looked down to change the radio station then you would prob-ably miss it.

That afternoon, the caution with which we packed our chutes for the jump, made a solemn ritual. Brittle jokes were answered by jagged laughter. Steve's beautiful but bemused girl friend, Lynn, cooked a meal for us, which

29

we referred to as our 'last supper'. When it was over we filled our glasses and raised them to toast our venture.

'Everybody comes home,' I said.

'Right!' agreed Steve.

The five hundredth coin spun skyward and the first tumbler clicked into place as we turned the key. On the carved lid of Pandora's box the gremlins gambolled drunkenly. We swept them aside with a brush of the hand. Inside, a monster turned his warty head one way and the other, sightless eyes searching the darkness for intrusion. His taloned fingers scratched at the inside of the lid and our laughter drowned out the sound of this warning.

We all retired early to bed. The downpour was over and clouds hung like storm shrapnel in the moonlight, the rain-washed night air tasting crisp and clean. Inside the house, the silence was shot through from room to room with a dark filigree of tension. I dozed fitfully, my mind filled not only with thoughts of the physical danger which tomorrow would bring, but the nagging doubts about my courage.

Jumping from a structure is a feeling very different from jumping out of an aeroplane. Refusals are rare among military jumpers standing with full kit in a tight line. The aircraft – these days usually a C130 Hercules – is thundering along through the sky, the smell peculiar to the inside of a working aircraft, no cushioned seats or lighting, no more air conditioning than an open door and the wind rushing through. If military jumpers refuse it is usually when they come to the balloon jump – a cold, clinical test of nerve which every military parachutist is expected to undergo. The balloon, the instructor and the students are raised on a cable tethered to the back of a truck, and in the stillness and silence at eight hundred feet they are told one after the other to step over the edge. There is no danger, nothing out there for the chutes to run into; it is merely a test of courage. Soldiers descending to the attack are fair game for the bullets of their enemies. They are vulnerable while under canopy. To ensure that they are exposed for the minimum amount of time the army fixes their absolute bottom line of safety at eight hundred feet. On the following morning we would be jumping from less than half that height. Contemplating this fact I eventually managed to sleep.

. . . But even as they slept, black leather wings carved through the night to their door. Dice had been rolled for them in the darkness and now the stranger had come to collect . . .

31

3

Misguided Inspiration

Standing at the open window, I saw that it was as perfect a day as we could have wished for. Not a breath of wind stirred the branches; the whole, vast Devonshire countryside was still and calm. There is something quite special about being active so early in the morning in high summer. The dew and the smell of moist earth and pasture implore even the most mundane soul to be up and doing. The sweet unrest of Kenneth Grahame's 'Wayfarers All' in *The Wind in the Willows*.

We left the house at four-thirty as the sun lifted above the horizon. Everyone seemed calm and relaxed, but once the journey started, so the tension rose.

'You've got wind streamers?' I asked.

'Yeah, I checked. We've got everything,' Steve said.

'Film?'

'Yeah, everything.'

Passing through village after village where not even the farmers were awake, it was as if we were the only moving thing in all the land. It is a deeply conspiratorial feeling to know that, as you rush headlong to meet fortune, all around you others slumber. The wheel turns for them as it does for you, but by your own choice you force your destiny. In the weeks that followed, as explanations were expected from us, it occurred to me that this forced destiny is a road open for all to pursue, but those who choose it must accept the misunderstanding to which – as we were – they may be subjected. If you purposely endanger your own life in search of a thrill, you will leave most people doubting your sanity, and in retrospect they may be right.

It took just over an hour to reach the gorge. The copses which punctuated the cultivated fields grew closer together until we were driving along the edge of a dark forest. The road led up on to higher ground and suddenly we were winding along through the boarded-up village of Cheddar. Columns of white rock sprang up on either side, and trees grew from precarious footholds high above the road.

It is no wonder that the ancient Britons attached spirits and small gods to streams and monoliths. But if a standing stone houses a lesser deity, then a gorge or sheer cliff must be home to a far greater one. Every towering Olympus dwarfed us in sun-blasted limestone. The pagan soul in anyone is surely touched by the awe and wonder of nature's chaos.

Our tiny vehicle drove on between the four-hundred-foot walls until we were swallowed up and the sound of the engine became an insignificant whine deep in the shadows. Presently we came into a broad sunlit amphitheatre. On the left an open space of short grass and shattered boulders was surrounded by low trees and shrubs. Beyond them steps of rock led up in colossal semi-circles to the higher reaches of the gorge. Overhead hung a crystal sky the colour of crushed sapphires, and on our right stood the highest wall of vertical rock I had ever seen. Way up there the planet Earth simply finished and dropped away into space. I felt suddenly cold standing in its dark shadow. Far above, tiny black crows wheeled away from the cliff and to my dying day I shall remember the harshness of their screams rebounding from the chasm walls.

We checked our gear, and started off back down the road into Cheddar village where a tourist stairway led up to the top. A ten-minute walk up a wooded and steeply inclined path brought us out on to a gorse plateau upon which gigantic slabs of stone lay bleached and smooth. Down a craggy rockface and through some more trees we went until, breathless and sweating, we came to the small flat plateau at High Rock. Shrugging off my backpack, I crawled on my belly to the edge and peered over. Below me, our car was a tiny miniature, no bigger than a fingernail at arm's stretch.

We threw paper streamers, which fell straight down, indicating that all was still. No shifting air currents waited to smash us into the cliff-face. We all felt the acute tension. A parachute jump from a rock, and at such a low altitude, is something that few seasoned skydivers would even consider. We knew there would be no chance of firing off a reserve chute should the main canopy fail to open, or

34

open incorrectly. The black wall breathed an ancient malice upon us and commanded a deep respect.

If the unthinkable happened, and one of us hit the cliff before the parachute opened, he would surely die. Even to collide into it under an open parachute would almost certainly result in serious injury or death. If the chute hesitated during opening or failed to leave the jumper's back, then it would be five seconds from exiting the high rock plateau to an eighty-mile-an-hour impact on the tarmac below.

All three of us questioned our motives for being there on that bright sunlit morning. For me, the question had been answered miles back along the deserted road at every empty village through which we had passed. We too should have been sleeping, but we chose to wake, and now stood at the unmarked crossroads of our destiny. On the one hand was a light step into open sky, touching nothing but sunlight, defying our human limitations. On this road Icarus beckoned to us, but on the other lay only ruin, appalling injury and death. If I had listened I might have heard the black velvet wings gliding into the shadows. Instead I saw only the crows. Carrion birds, but too small to bother us.

'Well, what do you think?' Steve said from behind me.

'Jesus! It's real scary, but it looks good,' I replied. Steve peered at me, genuinely concerned.

'Hey, look, it's not scary. It's no problem. Are you scared? Really?'

'Yeah. Yes, I'm really scared.'

We made ourselves busy with our preparations, hands working jerkily, breathing shallow. I wondered if the other two could possibly be as frightened as I was. Steve's words had sounded like bravado, but there he was, calm and controlled. I gave a deep sigh that belied the tightness in my chest.

*

The number one flight-training school at Brize Norton, in Oxfordshire, has a crest, resplendent in laurels and heraldic finery, beneath which the scroll proudly proclaims that 'Knowledge dispels fear'. I would suggest the author of this snippet of misguided inspiration be advised of one fact: he can never, ever, have been really scared. For when your soul is laid bare and there is nowhere to hide you will piss your pants regardless of what you know!

The sky was so clear and blue that talk of demons seemed hard to believe. But they were there – the fear, the doubt, and that terrible dying of spirit as courage falls to the onslaught of cowardice, though the latter certainly started ethereal antibodies to flow. Objectivity had yet to be learned, and before the true nature of our calling became clear first courage had to stand unguarded in the face of cowardice. Only with that experience could we become objective.

Of course pride can carry you a long way. When fear clouds objectivity, pride will spur you on. But then pride is one of the most jackass notions that a man can have.

While preparing for a cliff jump, one thing you are not short of is time. There is nothing to suggest you should jump as soon as you get there – though we were certainly intent on avoiding any public attention. One minute ran into the next, and soon there was just nothing else to be done. Steve was pushing.

'Okay, let's do it.'

36

That's a good way to get a job done; I've used that method in the years since Cheddar. Pushing does not allow you time to become frightened. Another way is to ignore what is happening until it is your turn to step over the edge. Just roll with it. Coast along on the wave of combined adrenaline. Do not ever think good or bad, or anything at all, until you have been checked and the cameras are rolling. It gives paranoia less of a chance to chisel at your strength.

One day I will sit in meditation on the very edge for an hour or so concentrating on this fear, imagining every second of jumping off, falling away and hitting the hard unforgiving ground, bursting and dying. Then, holding that image in fine focus, I will stand up and jump with open arms. This would be a complete negative of how we conducted ourselves that day, and every bit as untrue, though I suspect that ours was the easier way.

We knew that without a reserve option the jump had to be perfect in every detail on the first attempt. Even the simplest of mistakes could prove fatal. Complacency kills – and though we charged into our task, we made no apologies to each other for last-minute caution.

We had decided on our jump order the night before. Terry, being a less experienced jumper, gladly opted to be dispatched on a static line. So Steve would go first, then Terry while I assisted with his static line, and I would follow, jumping freefall.

When exiting from an aeroplane, a jumper quickly learns to use the windstream from the forward movement of the aircraft to maintain a stability in the fall. It feels almost exactly like riding a motorcycle at speed, a uniform and symmetrical airflow around you, holding you from falling forward. On a cliff jump you are falling into still air. There is no aerodynamic law which applies; it is a gymnastic movement, just like belly-flopping from the side of a swimming pool or on to a trampoline. In this situation there is practically nothing that a jumper can do to correct the position of his body if it becomes unstable. If you roll on to your back in freefall after leaving an aircraft, you can arch your body and the airflow will flip you over on to your front, to face the earth, but when jumping from a static object you will stay on your back.

With only four seconds to impact at Cheddar, it was essential to activate the parachute almost immediately, and the likely result would be entanglement with the rigging lines. This could affect the opening and even impede it. All this happening at approximately sixty miles an hour, ten feet away from the rockface would place us in more danger than anyone could hope to evade. We could be hurt. Terribly.

I went to a parallel outcrop and watched Steve step down on to the exit point.

*

There was no run-up here, just cold poised exit. Steve was standing on a triangular boulder and his toes overhung the edge slightly. Bolt upright on the brink of the chasm, he stood looking out to the opposite side; before him was a void, a yawning abyss which silently waited. He kept his face up from the view beneath his feet, and if he looked down then he did not tilt his head. Had he glanced into the gorge he might have seen something that the rest of us could not. Suddenly his whole tense frame became supple and I knew that his moment had found him. He looked across at me and with perfect control said, 'Right, I'm going now.'

'Have a good one,' I shouted, my face hidden behind the camera.

When Steve leapt from High Rock, he travelled up and straight out. In the instant of upward flight I fired the shutter. He hung for a split second, silent and weightless, while a few pebbles from under his feet skittered down the cliff. To us, in that moment, he surpassed the human, transcended fear and any shred of logic. Ten feet away from us, and in total silence but for the click of the camera, he froze in mid-air and then reality reached out to pluck him from flight.

As Steve peaked and fell so the five hundredth coin arched and dropped to earth. The last tumbler clicked into place and the die was cast. Miles back along the road somebody turned over, still sleeping.

In a tiny hamlet a crate of milk came crashing down outside a shop.

A door slammed in a back yard somewhere.

And the coin came clattering down, tails up and guilty for all to see. The lid burst open and rearing up from its prison rose the slavering monster, the carrion man, come to rend and tear.

As Steve dropped away his body started to arch downward until he was in a complete head down position a few feet away from the wall. Breathlessly we watched the backpack burst open as he rocketed down over the cliff face. His legs started to go over the top as the canopy and lines snaked past them. Two seconds away from impact and about half-way down, the chute reached the end of its rigging lines and crashed open. Immediately it surged forward into the shadows and I realised that Steve was flying, face first, straight into the rock. He disappeared beneath the overhang and I was given a brief glimpse of the tiny figure in the yellow T-shirt, kicking wildly and frantically, and pulling on the steering lines, two hundred feet above the ground, dwarfed by the rockface into which he was drifting.

Once, while flying in a Cessna 182, waiting to exit, we had cause to fly straight toward a wall of black cloud, a cumulo-nimbus with enough water in it to outweigh a battleship. At ten thousand feet it reached as far down as I could see and towered above us for another fifteen thousand. A five-mile high black-hearted thunderstorm, boiling and cracking. The air currents inside could literally have snapped a jumbo jet in half and the pilot of our tiny Cessna was understandably anxious for us to leave so that he could get back to the ground. In essence Steve had flown straight into much the same thing.

On the plateau it was utterly silent, but far below we could hear our friend being smashed again and again into the wall. Pitiful cries and gasps rose up to us as we stood ashen-faced high above. Then there was silence, and finally a single solid thump, and we knew that Steve was lying smashed and bleeding, possibly dead, in the shadows below.

We ran along the rim of the cliff, leaping from boulder to boulder, craning out in search of our companion.

'He's hit it. Jesus Christ, he's hit it!'

All three of us had known what the risks were but had refused to believe that they might affect us. Thinking of ourselves as indestructible we had coasted along, rejecting negativity with a curse, lionhearts who would gamble the last breath in our bodies. Suddenly reality dropped like a bottle in the dark.

From a flat overhanging boulder I could lean far enough out to see Steve lying at the foot of the wall. He was spreadeagled face down in the dust with his parachute covering his legs and spilling out across the road. I cupped my hands and screamed down at him, desperately hoping that he would respond.

'Steve! Steve, can you hear me?'

He turned his head to face the wall. At least there was some movement.

'Steve!'

I waited, and as the echoes died I could faintly hear a response. Terry looked at me,

'Oh, Jesus! Oh, Jesus Christ.'

We could do one of two things. I could follow Steve over the edge, and would be there to help him within seconds, despite my resolve being more than a little shaken by this slap in the face. The alternative was to run along the top of the gorge and climb back down into the village, then run up the road to the cliff. I leaned over and shouted.

'I'm coming down to you!'

Some indistinct words croaked up to us. The way along the cliff edge would take twenty minutes or so and Steve needed first aid now. I turned to Terry.

'What do you think?'

'I don't know.' He looked from me to the edge and shrugged nervously.

'Hell! I'm going for it,' I said. 'You don't have to jump. I'll see you down there.'

Steve and I had shared some extraordinary times and I

thought of him as one of those special friends one meets only once in a lifetime. Yet I felt a strange detachment. Perhaps we had after all accepted the consequences as well as the risks. In that moment when Steve left the cliff edge I knew he had achieved his goal. The challenge was met and I felt for and shared with him the supreme fulfilment which only commitment can bring. When the canopy took him into the wall, it could not mar his achievement.

Commitment, fulfilment, achievement – those were our reasons for being here, and so, after a moment's hesitation, I stepped down on to the exit rock and prepared to follow him. Behind me the sun had risen to full day. Ahead lay the gorge, warm and bright. There were no shadows this time for the carrion man had feasted and flown. I flexed my toes, feeling the edge so recently quit by another's feet. Visions of the tiny flailing figure engulfed in a limestone thunderstorm came flooding back but were beaten aside. There was no longer doubt, for purpose develops its own momentum which can neither be hurried nor hidden from. There was not a breath of wind, no birdsong. The Kamakura school of Zen has a sound for grass growing and a sound for hair turning grey. Only these things could be heard.

Finally leaving the rock was a blissful relief. It was as if my consciousness had jumped momentarily before my body, for as the solid frame leans forward it remains fixed by gravity. Even while your trailing foot is still in touch with the mountain there comes a point where balance is passed and equilibrium screams for justice. Here is the climax, for as nature reaches to pull you earthward you defy her, you power up and out, and it does not feel human.

The first time I looked down was after falling about sixty feet. That is almost two seconds of freefall and passing through forty miles an hour. It was an eerie perspective and one which, but for Steve, only dead people had seen. The tops of the trees and rocks came rushing up at me. It was like the view down from a tower block but here no rail immunised me from the fall and I was plunging those hundreds of feet. Being fired at the hard ground, my stomach felt soft and vulnerable. Steve was directly beneath me, in the centre of my impact zone. Time reeled past, and two hundred feet above the rocks I knew that if my parachute did not open in the next second then I would be smashed like a china doll.

Slowly the uncaring fabric lifted off and my backpack became supple. Fear clamoured at folly as my peripheral vision caught the blur of grey rock flashing past on either side. Doubt gave way to panic. The individual lines of Steve's canopy were now visible as I closed on him at seventy-five and still accelerating. His eyes, wild and staring, gazed up at me. I dropped into shadow, and in that moment was jerked viciously upright. With my mind working lightning fast, I reached for the control lines and looked up to check the canopy. It was flying clean and on heading, the awesome expanse of the wall, frighteningly close, now retreating slowly away from me.

I had made it. Nothing could harm me now. Two hundred square feet of nylon crashing open inside the gorge had made a sound like thunder, but I was leaving the thunder and the storm behind. As I flew out from the shadow of the cliff the canopy seemed to explode into dazzling brilliant light. All around and hurtling past came a hundred screaming crows fleeing from the awe of it.

Flying high above the ground, I too was screaming – in exhilaration. Moments later I touched down on a patch of short grass that was wet with dew. The canopy deflated and spread itself on the ground around me.

Shrugging out of the harness, I ran to where Steve lay. He was close to unconsciousness.

'How are you doing, mate? Where does it hurt?' I said breathlessly.

'I can't feel my legs,' he gasped. 'I've hurt my back! Fuck it hurts.'

'Don't worry,' I said, trying to reassure him. 'We'll get you patched up.'

As I began to check him over a loud crash made me duck down. High overhead Terry's canopy cracked open and I watched as he took control. The chute cleared the wall and went soaring across the gorge, flashing sunlight two hundred feet above us.

Anxiously, I waited as he guided the canopy out over the landing site. Suddenly, in my head, alarm bells were ringing.

'He's too hot,' I muttered to Steve. Then I was on my feet and shouting.

'Too hot! Lose height, you're too hot!'

Terry had been too hasty in getting his chute over the landing zone and was in danger of overshooting. At a hundred feet he was already half-way across the open area of grass. Now the opposite side of the gorge loomed over him, dwarfing the twenty-one-foot span of his canopy once again. At fifty feet he flew under the shadow of the opposite cliff, having completely overshot the landing site. With the options of a frontal impact on to the rockface at fifty feet or a low hook turn at thirty miles an hour in nil winds on to boulders with razor edges the size of cars, he chose the latter. Mercifully he was lost to our sight at the last second.

I stood in the centre of the road and stared open-mouthed, shaking my head in disbelief. Behind me Steve started a low moan – a horrible thing to hear, like the sound of an animal in unbearable suffering. I glanced back to see him lowering his face, pale and drawn with pain, into the dust. He had seen enough.

We had been spared the sight but not the sound of our friend being dashed and broken. It reached us from a hundred feet away – a heavy loud thud and, simul-taneously, an exhalation of breath forced out by the impact. A pall of dust rose over the spot. The canopy was stretched tightly over some larger rocks where the body had been catapulted away to line stretch. As silence descended once more in the gorge I pounded up the slope and across the open space. For the second time that morning, I fully expected to find a corpse lying among the stones.

Terry, when I reached him, was in an appalling state. His arms, legs and face were cut, bruised and bloodied. Thick blood was spattered across his forehead and his hair. His mouth was encrusted with stone chips, flaps of skin and dust. So violent had been the impact, that his jeans had split from mid-thigh, clean down through the hem, to lie in tatters around him.

4

Bristol and the One-thirtieth

One and a half hours after the carnage at Cheddar we were in the Bristol Royal Infirmary. It was the first of August and in the busy hospital we made a sorry trio.

'Yes, of course I was scared . . . who wouldn't be?'

'Was that the reason then?'

'No. No, not at all. I don't like to be scared.'

The rationalising started as the Pethidine took effect.

'I bet you wish you'd stayed in bed this morning.'

'No way! Hey look, it's a fools and heroes routine, right? The winners are heroes and the losers are fools. It doesn't matter. It's only that way because the people who are talking don't understand; they don't know what they are looking at. Win some, lose some. It was your turn to have the good luck this morning, that's all.'

'If I'd thought what we were doing at Cheddar was

46

down to luck,' I said, 'then I wouldn't have come.'

One of the nurses accused us of death-wishing but we argued the opposite. We spoke with passion of 'the feeling' of control over such stark fear, how for an instant everything had just faded away and there had been nothing left but oneself.

'It's the same with anything a person has a passion for, you know? It's the passion to live.'

When I returned to the airfield that night I wanted only to sleep. The day had been a long trial and already the trip to Cheddar seemed hazy and difficult to recall. Was it really only this morning that we three, happy and excited, had driven into the arena below High Rock? The passion to live which had been so finely focused then was now a blurred image and I stumbled into the building, weary and exhausted. What should have been the triumphant return of three adventurers was reduced to that of one, pitiful and shocked. I was among friends but could find nothing to say. Fifty miles away, Steve and Terry were still in the hospital, patched together with tape and plaster, and all I wanted now was to be taken in.

After sleeping for ten hours I awoke fully refreshed. The sun had risen on another cloudless morning and I looked forward to making some more conventional jumps. People started to arrive, loads on the aircraft were organised, and it was not until lunchtime that I was summoned into the office. There I was told to go straight away to pack my belongings and quit the drop zone by sunset. I was to stay away until further notice, possibly for good. Word had travelled fast and a decision had been reached in my absence. I may have taken a revolutionary step forward by successfully freefalling three hundred and sixty feet from the top of Cheddar Gorge, but that was one thousand six hundred and forty feet lower than the rulebook allows.

*

For the next month I wandered through the summer farmland in exile and passed the time away, pitching my tent on a hillside one night and in a forest the next. I moved further west until I came to a small airfield with a narrow grass landing strip and a single cabin for an office, where a good friend of mine from some years back ran a parachute school. There I stayed a while and toyed with the idea of working for an instructor's rating at his club. There was no accommodation to speak of however, and with the nights starting to grow colder, I bid him and the tiny airstrip farewell and hitched my way east again.

At another bigger airfield, I settled down and started work as a handyman for a local publican. I would get out of my tent when the sunlight woke me, wash at the airfield and then walk down to the inn to start work. By ten o'clock the aircraft would come roaring overhead and, just as soon as I had worked enough hours to pay for one jump, I would tidy up and return to the airfield.

I was asked to build a kennel extension for the publican's black labrador, which was about to have puppies. Judging by the size of her, there would be about twenty of them, and they would have to be contained until the publican managed to sell them off. There was no proper timber and the only tools he could provide were a rusty saw and a hammer with a shaft broken so short that half the time I ended up hitting the nails with my fist.

As all businessmen know, time is money, and as all

tramps know, money is food. That small job kept me in food, beer and skydives for two weeks while the labrador got fatter and fatter until she could have won a rosette as a prize Friesian at one of the local shows. She would waddle out each morning, let out a heavy sigh, and flop down on the doorstep to watch me. I felt a little guilty for working so slowly but I needed the money more than she needed the extra kennel space.

In the event, her timing was impeccable, though I'm not sure about her addition. She seemed to have given birth to more mouths than she had teats, though some could have been rabbits sneaking in for a hit. Every time I looked into the pen there were more things furry or feathered squawking and yelping and jumping around – puppies, kittens, rabbits, even a chicken or two. Eventually they organised escape committees and a good half of them hopped, strutted, or bounded away into the surrounding countryside, via cunningly concealed burrows and midnight gnawings at the wire.

The other dog of the house was called Nelson. He had earned a reputation by performing his trick on television. Live on the six o'clock news, the dog would balance a cookie on his nose, then on word of command he would flick the morsel high into the air and snap it up before it hit the ground. Village life was never the same again. Nelson had more street credibility than either Lassie or the talking terrier from BBC television's *That's Life*, whose vocabulary consisted of only the word 'sausages'.

Nelson the wonderdog was self-appointed guardian of the menagerie. Unfortunately Nelson was also one of the oldest living things left in the village, including the trees, and just like his namesake, the dog was fifty per cent blind. This made his cookie act the more impressive, but it also meant that as a guard dog he sucked. For whereas the Lord Admiral's blindness was restricted to all of one eye, the dog's was equally distributed between the two.

*

Late in the summer the countryside became a riotous tumble of foliage. The roadside ditches disappeared into hidden tunnels under the ferns and nettles, through which elusive creatures scrambled among the leaves. Butterflies flickered their gaudy display erratically along the hedge-rows and the roads became narrower than they had been in winter. On the winding lanes cars had to pull in to allow others to pass. Water was plentiful and the air humid from the jungle of tall undergrowth that crowded every untended space.

Of course, people knew that I had been one of the ill-fated Cheddar Gorge skydivers and now and then I would be questioned about it, though the questions were invariably prompted by sensationalism. 'Did you really jump off straight after your friend had hit the rock? Wow!' These people did not want to know our reasons for making the cliff jumps. They wanted only to hear about daredevils and injury, and so my philosophy, like their adulation, was wasted. But in time I managed to outlive the madness that had been Cheddar.

Among my skydiving companions at that time was an instructor named Alex Brown, who trained student para-chutists in Bristol and brought them to the airfield on Saturdays to jump. Alex's students would arrive from the city most weekends with a party of friends and relations, one of whom was a girl called Pat. She was pretty and very friendly. She had an effervescence which was over-whelming. Pat could go from wild laughter to genuine compassion in the space of a heartbeat, and when we talked about the disastrous cliff jumps, she showed a concern I had not seen before and was one of the few who did not ask ignorant questions. Such understanding from one so vivacious entranced me. We started a weekend acquaintanceship, which grew until, finally, I returned with her to Bristol one Sunday. After that I too became a weekend visitor to the airfield while living once more in close proximity to the Cheddar Gorge.

*

In Bristol I found myself with time on my hands. I had been camping out in fields and woods for so long that city life was something of a novelty and I spent a few days just walking round, taking in the sights. The Clifton Suspension Bridge was my favourite haunt. I would stand there for hours, looking down along the length of the Avon Gorge where climbers dotted the cliff faces, thinking over the events which had led me to this place. Sometimes the tollman would come past to see what I was up to. With suicide leaps common, it must have made him wary to see the same person come and stand in the middle of the bridge for a few hours each day.

Mankind has always attached importance to high places. They hold an irresistible fascination for most people, and also provide security and defence to those who can see the furthest. The thrill of gazing down as though suspended in the air can have other effects too. I am sure that some people must have thrown themselves to their deaths simply because they gazed too long and an instant madness took them. Sometimes, when looking down from the roof of a building or the stairwell of a fire escape, I find myself fighting this madness, gripping the edge with knuckles grown white in subconscious desperation. But the bridge was a pleasant place for thinking and I enjoyed the feeling of being perched up there with all that empty space under me.

Escaping unscathed from the Cheddar jumps had filled my spirit and I felt strong within. Yet the whole mad whirlwind of it was unbalanced in my vision. On the one hand was the exhilaration of an out-and-out glory day in which we had been the ones to show the courage, or stupidity, to go and try it; on the other was the fact that the venture had resulted in such chaos – and, of course, the smugness of our detractors' 'we told you so'. Both Steve and Terry were whole again and working at their old drop zone. They escaped my penalty for they had been established long before I came to spend the summer there. Without the company of these friends I grew broody.

Clinging to companionship is a trait which we find both in children and less obviously in adults. While relatively helpless in a world whose decisions are beyond its ken, a child must cling to the safest place, firstly its mother. As it begins to grow stronger the child will explore the tribe and, like attracting like, will normally find a group with which to ally itself. Then, as responsibility starts to weigh more heavily, the youngster will mature and learn to find security from within. With the time dilution which the structured planning of adult life demands the 'now' living of our carefree childhood is left behind.

Psychiatric patients experiencing deep regression under

hypnosis have been known to pass into other states of consciousness in which they can recount tribal or even animal characteristics of their own past. This 'freeing of the spirit' is called atavism. It is the joy felt by children playing or by animals leaping and chasing. It is the forgotten pleasure of living the moment, of existing in the 'now' timeframe.

Of course the exhilaration of this 'now' living does not prepare one for accidents. You will not see a parachute malfunction coming, but when it arrives your actions must be swift and decisive if injury is to be avoided. Mistakes are the fault of the injured. The one saving grace here is that accident usually strikes so fast that fear and pain are not immediately apparent. I can remember that when I was an amateur boxer a tingle of fear was the normal prelude to each fight. Yet as soon as the bell rang and we started to trade punches, fear had no place. All one's time was taken up in dealing with the situation – block that punch, weave right and fire a jab, roll left and try a hook to the head. Fear comes first, then action, and lastly pain. Seldom are punches felt when they land, and least of all if they knock you down. In that moment there is just the all-encompassing feeling of 'where the hell am I?' While engaged in the actual combat one cannot waste time with fear. Reaction to the moment is the most important thing, and there is no fear or pain; just being.

It has been recorded under laboratory conditions that the quickest time for a fit and healthy person to respond to external stimulus is one-thirtieth of a second. This applies to anything from a loud sound making you jump suddenly to a bright light causing the pupil of the eye to contract. At Clifton Bridge I came to believe that by our actions at Cheddar we had brought ourselves close to that fraction of a second, and therefore closer to the atavistic 'now'. The 'fine madness' that I had predicted before the cliff jumps was – unknown to me – one so primal that it mocked at reason. The passion to live which I had found there would not be denied. When we had stood on the edge, nothing else had mattered, and our thoughts were fixed on the moment. To step off and plunge downward was so 'now' that it felt like crossing beyond that thirtieth of a second. This return to 'now' was the forgotten state, the 'feeling' about which each of us had spoken.

We had visited the one-thirtieth and found chaos. Now its memory called me back to settle the score. What I thought of as a celebration of 'now' was marred by accident, and in my naïvety I presumed this to be negative, not seeing that the blood and pain were just as much a celebration of being as the sunshine and exhilaration. Truly deluded, I had allowed the prejudice of my own mortality, and the deep-rooted tribal desire for endurance, to attach more value to the outcome than to the act itself.

At the time, this delusion was absolute. To assess the lesson of experience we need to find a focal point, and I was still too close to make perspective work. The lid of Pandora's box had been replaced firmly, with the monster shackled once more within. I still possessed the key, but my victory seemed to have been by slim chance. The thought of using the key again made me shiver. In the throes of this uncertainty I spent many long hours on the edge of revisited chaos. I could have hurled the unwanted key down from the rail of the bridge at any time, but it was as if I stood in a doorway, and while I remained on the threshold the door could never be totally closed.

*

The weeks flew by in Bristol as summer gave way to the low skies and russet leaves of autumn. Pat and I remained together while I scratched a living by packing parachutes at the drop zone. We shared a fondness for whisky and coke and would sometimes drink by candlelight in Pat's large and spacious kitchen. One night, while we were sitting at home, there came a knock at the back door. It was our friend Alex, come to pay us a visit. The flickering candles threw a huge distorted shadow of him on the wall as Pat welcomed him in. I fetched another glass and poured Alex a drink as he sat down beside me. It was a scene of friendship and warmth as the silhouette of autumn's first naked branches swayed on the curtain in soft candlelight that did not reach into the far corners of the room.

While we talked, we became aware that Alex had brought with him a companion. Whirring around the candle like a leaf possessed by demons, a large brown moth wheeled and circled.

'Why do they do that?' I said over my glass.

'They can't help it,' said Pat. 'It's a madness.'

'You should know about that,' Alex added. He likened our endeavours at Cheddar Gorge to the moth's senseless possession.

'No, it's really not the same thing,' I said. 'We had it planned out. Things just got a little out of hand.'

'Well, yeah, but this guy here,' – Alex gestured to the

moth – 'he doesn't actually mean to get burned either, you know. But, as Pat says, it's a madness, and he just can't help coming back.'

'That's right,' said Pat. 'To moths, flames are beautiful, and they have to get closer. It isn't something which they can control.'

Those words stayed with me long after Alex had left and Pat and I had retired to bed. I lay there, half sleeping, and thought over the significance of what he had said. Perhaps night vision is the prize of those who prefer the darkness. Certainly the flame had burned so brightly for us at Cheddar that I was now left groping blindly. No 'piper at the gates of dawn' healed me with his magic. No will-o'-the-wisp beckoned me to follow.

Pilgrim's feet turn bewildered and old night draws her black veil down.

I knew that soon I would have to return to London to assure myself of employment before the slack winter months started in earnest. The thought saddened me, but with my cash diminishing fast and autumn drawing on, the move seemed inevitable. Yet there still remained some unfinished business. Before leaving, I decided, the past adventuring had to be ended satisfactorily and I would enlist Pat's help that I might complete it. Pondering the options open to me, I glided into sleep, and if a blind moth crashed into the window that night, then I knew nothing about it.

5

The Soaring Spirit

Few would want to repeat those Cheddar Gorge jumps. Word of our adventure reached far and wide, but the catalogue of injury accompanying the tale ensured that no one stole our thunder.

When we drove into the amphitheatre, it was the timelessness that struck me, the indifference not just to our presence but to our very existence. Again the air was thick with crows, endlessly circling in the upper reaches of the gorge. I walked across the landing site and sat among the rocks. It was late September and cold at that early hour. The shattered tumble of limestone opposite was almost white in the morning sunshine. I squinted up at the black profile of the edge three hundred and sixty feet above me. While I watched the sun crept over the plateau and burst down upon me. The black wings of the crows glistened like lacquer as they soared away in the light.

Pat climbed with me up into the forest at the top of the gorge. As we picked our way along the edge to High Rock, images of the last time came crowding in. Now and then a faint rumble far below told us of an early-morning juggernaut winding its way through the ravine. The walls played tricks with the sound, so that we heard it crunching through the gears long after it had gone.

When finally we climbed down and pushed through the denser thicket on to the exit plateau, I felt suddenly calm. It was almost a homecoming, and eagerly I scrambled down to peer over the edge. The view from High Rock is staggering. Due to the circular rock steps on the opposite side, the gorge seems deeper than it really is. Far below, the tiny specks of the crows circled still, while their calls ricocheting in the amphitheatre drifted up to us.

Our cairn of three large rocks, erected in bravado to mark our feat on the last trip, lay scattered round about. Someone had kicked them over, possibly a climber – no one else would come to this place. I restacked them: it didn't matter, but from respect to my friends I felt obliged to do so. All those who undertake to visit these 'theatres of folly' – be they climbers, skydivers, hang-glider pilots or whatever – talk of a strange calmness which falls just before the moment of starting. In a storm of adrenaline and emotion there comes a moment when, suddenly, a cold unshakeable control is found. In later times it occurred to me that, though the adventurer cannot eradicate his fear, he learns to exercise a control over it. For though he will never become a friend, the familiar face of the carrion man no longer disturbs him.

Fear hides easily in the fabric of truth but, even in the

most fertile theatre, it is rarely justified and continuity is a great help in controlling it. After living through almost eleven thousand nights since birth I can still, if primed, lie in bed and darkly fantasise until fear makes me pull the covers closer. The protection afforded is as false as the demons imagined. It's fun to do this on occasion – to give your imagination a workout. But don't mistake it for the real thing. It can be pretty convincing, but it is nothing more than a cheap thrill.

Our perception of life is overlaid with illusion so that often we cannot see when we are loved, do not realise when anger or hatred cloud our judgment. Zen philosophy teaches the division of illusion and objectivity, and one of the terms frequently used in the teaching is *makumozo*, 'no delusive thought'. Anyone who has taken LSD and then had the room fill up with rotting zombies knows how convincing fear can be, but *makumozo* will tell you it's only the drug.

Adrenaline is the drug which our bodies secrete in order to cope with 'now' living. It is a substance which can be put into a test tube and analysed and, like most hard drugs, it is addictive. Once tasted, the prospect of the next fix is a powerful temptation. After several rushes your tolerance for it enables you to handle a larger amount, until eventually your attention wavers and you fall to an overdose. You have been moving towards it with sure direction and never once has it announced its presence. It overcomes you without warning and there is no escape. When one night the flesh-eater climbs in through your window and rips the covers from your bed, you may raise a finger in defiance or you may soundlessly surrender to oblivion, but one thing will be certain: whatever you do, it will make no difference at all. Silence rules the graveyard. This does not mean that you may not whistle, but don't think that whistling will save you from the thing that stirs in the mould, should the nightmare come to you.

Fear on a BASE jump usually peaks and then stops. It is as if the jumper becomes tired of waiting for the monster to appear. Or maybe it is the realisation that we have stated our intention and would now rather risk bodily injury than lose our spirit blood by backing down. Objectivity safeguards us from this emotional folly by enabling us to assess the conditions, the site and any contributing factors, and fix the probability of success or failure. If the calculation brings us to the conclusion that the only barrier to realising our goal is a shortcoming of courage, then we are bound to action.

Still, on this bright new morning my spirit was soaring, and from the moment I dragged on my chute I felt good about the jump. It was as though the time lapse since our last visit had washed the area clean of any malice it held. The sun-blasted wasteland, as bleak before as the mountains of the moon, was now warm and cheerful. I stepped down on to the smooth, flat exit rock. Looking at it, and then beyond to the tops of the trees far down on the other side, I wondered how many people had fallen before me unassisted.

Standing there, close up against the edge, you cannot see the wall itself. Something inside dares you to look, but to lean forward and glance down the face to the foot of the rock is more than courage will allow. So I stood in the early morning sun, staring out to the wooded slopes four hundred feet up on the opposite side, and never looked down until I had left the edge. 'Nobody goes unstable. Nobody goes unstable.' Again and again I repeated it, trying to convince myself. Later, at the house, Pat said that she could hear me mumbling something, but was unable to catch the words.

In the silence I took that one irreversible step – and dropped like a stone. Deep in the muscle of my heart the blood pounded. My brain rebelled against the information it was given. My senses shifted to place the feeling. Logic fled screaming as a wave of fear broke over me. Ten paces to my left I heard the loud click and whir of the camera. I feasted on the illusion that the wall soaring past was actually the ground and that I was flying along it. Bushes on the rockface were shrubs and trees that I was flying over.

On a low-altitude jump, once you have activated your equipment by throwing out the pilot chute to pull the main canopy from your back, there is nothing more you can do. A reserve activation in the event of the main chute failing is not an option left open to you. With four seconds to impact, it would take you most of the fall to pull the main and then to realise what was happening – or not happening – and to open your reserve. There would simply not be enough air time left. So, having kicked off and thrown the pilot, I just waited while hammering down the cliff face directly over the roof of the car.

I had the awful feeling that I hadn't launched strongly enough. My skin crawled with the sensation of being far too close to the wall. I bent my knees at as tight an angle as I could for fear that the rock skimming past would touch my feet. Then, when I could plainly see through the sunroof of the car the map book resting on the driver's seat, the canopy crashed open, jerking me upright and blasting the breath from me.

I was ecstatic, though the opening had been very low, below a hundred feet. Accelerating towards the ground at one hundred and four feet per second, I had feared the gorge was about to claim me for another victim. With no time to release the control lines from their keepers, I landed in the road at the foot of the wall, pitching forward into the dust at the roadside. Immediately I was on my feet, screaming and howling with the release of pressure. The air above was filled with angry screaming crows and through the centre of the boiling flock, higher still on the cliff edge, a tiny figure waved down at me.

A movement attracted my attention and I saw someone running towards me from the rocks beyond the road. Wide-eyed and open-mouthed, the man threw out his hand for me to shake. I took it and in the same instant saw over his shoulder a red van at the foot of the wall, with a woman standing beside it cradling a baby.

'Man!' he shouted, 'Oh, *man!*'

'Hey, did you enjoy that?' I said, gathering my chute and grinning insanely. He looked like a left-over hippie, all long beard and wooden beads.

'Well, I've been living in this van for fifteen years,' he said, 'and I have never seen anything like that!'

6

Winter in a Blank City

The return journey to Pat's house was far less solemn than the outward trip. I dropped my gear down on the living-room floor, Pat opened a bottle of champagne and we celebrated the successful jump. A BASE jump always seems to have been easy when you are safely looking back on it. I recalled the reaction of our unexpected onlooker and we laughed as we imagined him driving from place to place and telling his story. Pat joked that we should set up shop in the gorge and sell tickets to spectators.

It may have been due to the champagne, or more likely the rush of adrenaline that pounded through my veins, but the idea did not seem ludicrous. If the response we'd seen at Cheddar was anything to go by, people might be willing to pay to watch stunt parachuting. Our enthusiasm grew and soon our imaginations began to run riot as we dreamed of photographs for roadside billboards and eye-catching advertisements for sportswear, or television commercials of a skydiver leaving the fifty-second storey window of a big London bank, with the voiceover intoning 'when you need a little help . . . ' and then the parachute crashing open with the company logo painted across it. Before long we were taking the idea seriously.

Over the next few weeks we had letterheads and business cards printed, and set up a bank account in the name of 'Captain Jaques' Flying Circus – Stunt Parachutists'. I wrote articles for magazines and newspapers and duly sent them off with photographs for consideration. We contacted television studios and suggested live coverage of more cliff jumps. I even wrote to the trustees of the Clifton Bridge for permission to organise a parachuting event there. Everybody wished us well but nobody wanted to become involved. At best we were treated with amusement, and sometimes we were ignored. The newspapers said they had seen it all before; the TV companies had better things to do; the commodity suppliers thought it too risky to lend their names to such games. They all hoped that we would find success elsewhere.

By the middle of November the Flying Circus had become a pile of unused stationery and a folder packed with stillborn dreams, and our bank balance was down to one pound. The world, it seemed, was too busy to spend time watching lunatics. Not a glimmer of interest had been sparked by our enthusiasm. Unlike skydiving, BASE jumping is a viable spectator sport, but the world is seasoned with sanity, and where once the shock of the new was marked by fleeting attention, now shock is the

Securing the static line
and preparing to jump
at Cheddar Gorge

Being fired at the hard
ground, my stomach felt soft
and vulnerable

Taking that one irreversible step for a second time at Cheddar Gorge

Leaving the cliff at Beer Head in Devon, 300 feet above the sea

The 1,050-foot TV mast at Mendelsham

order of the day. While Steven Spielberg has got the
water into wine routine off pat, Saatchi and Saatchi must
have something more up their sleeves than a crucifix with
'coming soon' stamped across it.

*

Autumn was by now cocooned in crisp leaves, awaiting
the emergence of winter, and fields of burned stubble lay
more dead than dormant. Black boughs, like the shadows
of lightning bolts, pierced the sagging clouds and held
them painfully on Daliesque stilts. Skydiving in the
winter time is not a sport for the faint-hearted. Twenty-
five degrees below zero outside the aircraft is by no means
uncommon and an in-flight door is a luxury not always
available. The rigor mortis effect of falling through two
miles of this bracing air, however, does numb the pain of
landing on hard frozen ground. In winter a drop zone
operates with a skeleton staff and bad weather can mean
that people on courses are ground trained but often never
jump. The rich pickings of summer fell away like the
leaves from the trees, and I knew that it was time to head
home. Bristol reserved what occupation it had for its
natives and there was no room for outsiders. In London,
though, opportunity beckoned and any man willing to
work could find reward.

It was with a sad farewell that I left Bristol. Pat drove
me down past the yachts at the quayside to the rail
terminal at Temple Meads under a dark and thundery sky.
The gargoyles on the old gothic buildings around the
university frowned at us and the magnificent swoop of
the cables at the bridge were as breathtaking as ever. We
managed to say goodbye in the station without a tear

for we both knew that it was time, and in any case I had no real choice. As I sat on the train, waiting to leave, memories of the summer's events drifted past like ghosts. Even now, six years later, a picture of Clifton or the mention of things dear and familiar about the area can make me smile. In my exile, Bristol had taken me in and been kind to me.

Looking back, I had no regrets. I had experienced much that I would never forget. I felt sad when I recalled the injury to my friends, I felt sad too at the negative reaction of our peers. They had always said that BASE jumping was unsafe and that to attempt it was dangerous; now they chose to ignore the successes and pointed instead to the bloodshed. For me Cheddar Gorge had become a ragged scar.

*

When I arrived in London, my first impression was that everything was a lot taller and moved a lot faster. Whereas in Devon the spectacle of life is played out and watched on a small village green among rolling farmland, here in London it is set in a huge stadium, where cruel spectators wreak effortless destruction or inspire the collective conscience to mark change by the whim of their thumb. Here the battling dinosaurs of enterprise are in tournament, while small businessmen merely cause the manic pulse to quicken. In this mêlée of snatch and grab, where faceless legions are employed, work was easy to find. Though each individual was different, the people I laboured with formed just another demolition gang and together we were once more a part of the grey monster. As we say in the trade, same shit, different flies.

Sometimes I wonder if the people who come to pass in our vision, but with whom we have no dealings, are no more than 'blanks'. That once out of sight they sit and do nothing: they don't eat, or sleep, or watch television; they simply sit and stare at the wall until tomorrow morning, when they will drive past you again in the traffic. To you, who were we faceless ones you passed at the roadside, bare-chested and dirty? Who sat opposite you on the last train you rode? We are all grey men, for I could never draw your face.

On his enlightenment Buddha was heard to announce: 'In heaven and earth I alone am the chosen one.' Meaning, as far as I can tell, that his life was his to lead, and that the same goes for everyone else. But then, after all he was deified, so even if Buddha had said, 'What the bloody hell are you all staring at?' it would hardly have mattered. Just like those devotees in *Monty Python's Life of Brian* who saw Brian's every misguided step as divine, someone would have found an interpretation to justify it.

Once we realise that we are each other's blanks, then we can find both humility and compassion. I might feel proud to have jumped from a building or a cliff, and yet in a crowded bar I stand anonymous. But if I have done this, and so easily taken grey cover, it may be that the blank next to me has just returned from a distant war, soloed the Eiger or canoed the treacherous Sun Kosi.

*

The following spring found me teetering along the same beams and trapezes of a year before. The Flying Circus lived on in memory, and sometimes a Circus card would be handed out as a keepsake or curiosity. Finding myself still banned from skydiving in the west country, I broke north to a new location. It was a good move. With a larger aircraft permanently on the airfield, bigger and more ambitious freefall link-ups could be perfected and the state of the art grew swiftly to new heights. Things of which I would not have dreamt now became everyday occurrences as I flew in harmony with my new-found companions two miles or more above the ground.

This new drop zone lay outside the tiny thatched village of Pampisford, near Cambridge. Here, individual expression was not discouraged and jumpers from all over England came to skydive in the relaxed atmosphere. Attempts were made to secure freefall formation records at the club. One windy cloudswept afternoon at the beginning of summer, twenty female jumpers teamed up to take the British all-women's record.

Towards the end of the year a European night record was attempted. The official world record for a formation put together at night was twenty-seven, but the figure in Europe was lower. If we could put sixteen people into the sky at night above the English countryside, it would be a European record. To this end, twenty-six of us gathered at the nearby Cranfield parachute centre, and I well remember the nervous prelude to climbing aboard and the biting cold of the ride to altitude . . .

7

Flying by Moonlight

We were flying at thirteen thousand feet, and I was sitting next to the open door. The jump was scheduled – as most night jumps are – to coincide with the full moon. The aircraft was filled to capacity, and even the fuel weight had been taken into consideration to ensure that we had enough runway to get airborne. Now twenty-six of us waited for the radar at Stanstead to assist the pilot in finding the airfield again.

Night flights in small open aircraft are a sensual banquet. Five thousand feet below us a thin wispy layer of cloud reflected the strong moonlight. I could see another eight thousand feet below that through gaps in this lace curtain where twinkling groups of lights marked the villages and towns. A lake or reservoir somewhere down in the darkness held the mirrored image of the moon faintly through the furrows of silver. Luminous spaghetti spilled across the countryside where motorways merged and split. The town of Milton Keynes was a breathtaking nebula of swarming electricity.

Above us stars were spattered across the darkness, and I knew that we would be almost invisible from the ground – a tiny aircraft heard only as a faint hum of engines high overhead. The discerning eye might pick out the red and green lights on each wingtip, or even the flashing beacon under the fuselage, but to most we would go unnoticed. Inside, the aircraft was dim, yet our vision had adjusted even before we had left the ground. No one on the load had been indoors for the last half hour before take off. Countless hot drinks had been ferried out to us as we stood waiting in the cold night for permission to board. Sixteen jumpers were to link up and secure the record, while a further eight of us carrying high-energy halogen lamps as we fell, would guide each of them out of the night to the formation. Two more skydivers would record the jump on stills, cine-film and video with a variety of cameras.

A square of moonlight travelled slowly across the floor as the pilot banked the plane. Each face was illuminated momentarily, some of us shielding our eyes from the glare. For a few seconds I sat with my feet on the very sill of the doorway, completely bathed in silver light, before the pilot completed his final turn in over the drop zone for the jump run and the moon disappeared behind the tail, throwing us all back into darkness.

Skydiving from aeroplanes usually held no fear for any of us – certainly not the mortal terror which had arisen from the black wall of Cheddar. Yet jumping at night on a European record attempt, and the exhaustive ground practice and lectures on what was expected from each diver, made for an added tension. Unlike Cheddar, the thrill was now enjoyable rather than threatening, and it was for that thrill that I loved to skydive. It was a confidence in my ability and my equipment that went all the way back to Captain Jaques and Eddie of the Skies, in a farmer's field in Devon.

There were several factors to be considered at the exit point. It was essential to get everyone out of the aircraft as close together as possible, so that all the jumpers had the maximum amount of time in which to build the formation. For this reason some of us would exit through the side door and the rest would dive out of the tailgate. My position was to hang on to the outside of the fuselage with one hand while holding the pistol grip of my halogen lamp in the other. When the exit command came, I was to flick the switch of the lamp and drop away pointing the light at the door and the underbelly of the plane. The cameramen exiting the tailgate at the same time would film the rest of the jumpers leaving the aircraft.

A mile out we stood up and started stretching our limbs, tightening straps and buckles on our equipment. Last-minute checks were made on the chute of the jumper in front while I stood on the edge of the side door looking out across the clouds and the lights thousands of feet beneath me. Outside the aircraft the night had a luminescence. Suddenly the order was passed down the line from the cockpit.

'Climb out.'

The tailgate lifted and was secured high up in the ceiling. The noise and the howling cold wind increased their intensity. The jumpers started to walk to the edge and peered at the lights far below.

I flattened myself against the trailing edge of the door and, gripping the ribbed interior of the fuselage, eased my way outside. The eighty-miles-an-hour propeller blast tried to rip me from the side, but with one foot left in the corner of the door and one hanging in space I was in position. With my right hand I held the door jamb and in my left the lamp, poised ready to light up the exit for the cameras. In the windrush I would not hear the exit command but the first man in line from the side door was to relay it to me before I acted.

It was essential that the lamps be switched off until the right moment so that night vision might be preserved for a successful jump. My lamp was equipped with a 250-watt bulb supplied by a heavy dry-cell battery carried inside my suit through wires fed down the left sleeve. These lamps were so taxing on the batteries that we could not be sure they would last until we landed. Once safely under our opened canopies, the lights would be turned off until we touched down.

It seemed a long time from climbing out to seeing a spectral hand appear in the doorway giving the thumbs up. I flicked the switch and dropped away on the cushion of the slipstream. The white underbelly of the skyliner thundered overhead as the tail sprinkled its human confetti into the darkness and then the glare of the lights.

After a couple of seconds, when I figured that the cameraman behind me must have filmed enough of the exit, I flipped through a hundred and eighty degrees to face him. Surfing like superman on the propeller blast, he sat up arms swept back, legs extended, firing off shots, the flash of his helmet-mounted camera clicking and whirring like a laser show. Over his shoulder other lamps were converging on a dark mass building against the silvery clouds below. I straightened my body, and rocketed past the cameraman, trying to gauge the distance and choose my position. When I was close enough to make out colours in the group I flew to my appointed area. The cloud was coming up to meet us, and as I started to edge in closer to the formation we hit it. It was like impacting on a snow-covered moonlit mountainside which parted soundlessly to let us through. Luckily the cloud layer was thin – only about five hundred feet – and within two and a half seconds we were through it and into clear sky again.

A complete circle of lamps now surrounded the formation, two thousand watts of light electrifying the air, the repeated flash of the stills camera like a lightning storm all around us. I didn't look at my altimeter, for it would be too dark to read it on the outside of the group. They would know in the centre when it was time to start thinking about saving bodies rather than securing records. With the task almost done, the last few jumpers swam out of the darkness beyond the circle and made their final approaches. When the last man came floating in and took his preplanned slot on the edge of the mat of falling bodies, finding his position in the cold moonlight, the group was completed and well over a ton of humanity went hurtling together at a hundred and twenty miles per hour through the night towards the glittering town below.

On my right, one of the cameramen, followed by a lamp bearer, flew gently down to the edge of the linked formation and flipped over on his back to fall away filming from below. Suddenly those in the middle were kicking their legs, the signal for us to disengage and go our separate ways. We were running out of altitude. The clouds were already almost a mile above us. I turned, swept my arms back to my sides and delta'd away across the sky like a shooting star.

Those on the ground could see nothing of the formation but the lamps swimming out of the aircraft like fireflies, grouping together in a circle like some kind of UFO, and now exploding away from each other as in a firework display. Only we knew that the jump had been successful, though soon enough everyone at the landing site could tell from the howling and screaming of jumpers under canopy that circled the landing area. Our friends ran out to meet us on a wave of congratulations, and with beer for everyone. Film of the event was immediately dispatched in waiting transport that would speed it away to television news agencies and the national papers. It was a new British and European night record at the first attempt.

*

We had taken daylight to darkness and by brute force had found accomplishment. But there are 'others' who walk unrecognised by day and don their true guise while the moon shines on blissful sleepers. For them the night is a blessed cloak of secrecy. They use the dreaming hours to meet their calling with less carnival than our full-scale assault. Night covers all kinds of less publicised endeavour and, in this way, does like attract like, unerringly bringing together dreamers, poets and madmen.

Skydivers are by nature a boisterous breed. A bar

frequented by jumpers is a loud sprawling circus where one can join in the tomfoolery or sit back and be entertained. It was on a summer's evening, almost one year after the blood on the rocks at Cheddar Gorge had dried, that a chance comment over a table at which I was sitting between two friends, triggered the wheel to uneasy movement once more.

I had met Kyle Ward and Dan Arlen through a mutual friend at the airfield. After my second successful jump at Cheddar a handful of other skydivers had made the leap from High Rock. These two men were among that small number and, captured by the same madness, they now spoke of a new goal. At a village called Mendlesham, which lay fifty miles to the east of us, was a television transmitter mast – a thousand-foot tower of iron girders supported by a spider's web of steel cables. Kyle and Dan were departing later that night secretly to scale the fence surrounding the pylon and to climb one thousand feet up the ladder into the darkness. In the first light of day they intended to jump from the top.

By the time we left the bar I had talked my way into their plan and arranged to rendezvous with them at three-thirty the following morning. We toasted our venture before leaving for our tents. As I raised the glass I saw myself in the bar mirror and was instantly reminded of an identical scene.

'Everybody comes home,' I muttered, more to myself than to my companions. The barman interrupted my thoughts by placing the change for our drinks down on the counter. Three coins, all heads up.

8

On the Dark Stairway

Up the dark stair go those in torment
While Thugee stranglers await the dusk.
Release them on to the night,
Release them into the darkness.
Glutting their pangas,
    to slake the goddesses thirst.

It was bitterly cold when I awoke. In the pitch darkness somebody had shaken me, a cracked voice whispered harshly of urgency. It was time to leave. Sleep hung upon me like a black veil from which I was loth to go. The night bore down, holding me on the threshold of slumber. I sat up, skin hardening with the cold. Outside the tent I could hear Kyle and Dan moving around. There came the sound of a tent zip fastener. A car door creaked open and a parachute harness jingled, clear and familiar in the stillness. Blindly I felt for my clothes and began to dress. Within fifteen minutes we three had slipped silently away.

In spite of what romantics will tell you, I have come to believe that each man is an island. We may build bridges or form archipelagos, there are clubs which we visit, but we are born alone, and will die in that manner. That is not up to us; it is the nature of life which is our choice. For that reason we had gone out into the darkness that night – to shout across the ocean and mark our islands. It was an hour's drive to the mast, and once we got moving anticipation started to accelerate me away from drowsiness. If I shut my eyes there was strange music emanating from within my head, tuneless and repetitive. I do not know the physiology of excitement or the chemical changes with which the body prepares itself for trial, but my chest felt tight so that breathing was difficult, and my feet were tapping rhythmically in the darkness behind the driver's seat.

Once again, as we sped through benighted villages, I revelled in the cloak of conspiracy. Even our own people back on the airfield were asleep, trailing through the dark passages of the night. We were about five miles from the mast when we got our first sight of it. A glimmer of red showed briefly through the trees to the east. Someone in the front of the car pointed it out, but it was already gone. Then, a minute later, far off in the night but unmistakable, we saw four red lights, one atop the other and sat up trying to see more. As we cleared the side of a small hill the ground to our right dropped away and we looked across to seven red beacons reaching high up into the starlight. Far away overhead, in the gaps between the stars themselves, the last red lights blinked lazily, silently, on and off.

But above the car, fifty feet up and a hundred feet out over the fields to our left, a forgotten enemy had been drawn to the tower. Sightless eyes in a gorgon head turned towards it and, croaking with excitement, the harpie banked hard to the right and went rocketing out to the foot of the ladder. He came low over the roof of the car, less than ten feet up, but was lost to us in the night. Oblivious to the creature, we too raced to the foot of the mast.

*

We stopped the car outside a small factory plant, adjacent to the pylon. At the back of the perimeter fence we were hidden from view and when we killed the lights and cut the engine the silence pressed in close. I stepped out of the car. It was very cold, and a faint glimmer of paler sky showed away to the east. On the ground all was calm, the stillness absolute. Yet underlying the silence, a faint rushing sound, almost a moaning, could just be detected. I turned my head this way and that, trying to pinpoint where it was coming from. Eventually I realised that the sound was above, high on the mast, where air was moving between the girders, giving eerie voice to the wind.

So conspiratorial was our mood that we spoke in low whispers, though the factory was deserted and no one was within earshot. A hundred yards away across the crop-field, the compound of the mast was a dazzling floodlit area which spilled out beyond the eight feet of barbed wire. Hoisting on our chutes, we started to pick our way between the rows of crops to the fence.

Scaling the barbed wire was easy and placed us inside the perimeter and close up against one of the buildings. The loud hum of generators was now apparent and I felt a tingle of fear. Doubt called me back from the darkness beyond the fence, but the time for second thoughts was long past. The final twenty feet to the pylon was an exposed area of shingle in full view of the compound windows. Peering round the edge of the building, I looked into a well-lit room which appeared to have been recently quit, for there were coffee cups on the table and newspapers to hand. Whatever strange tribe inhabited this world of tangled pipe and cable was evidenced by these *Marie Celeste* personal effects abandoned within the safe confines of their castle keep.

There was only one way to get on to the mast. Staring straight at the window I backed across the stones, horribly loud under foot, until my hand touched the concrete base of the structure. Then in one movement I turned and vaulted up into the cage of the pylon. Reaching high over my head, I found the ladder and swung out on to it. A ring of barbed wire circuited the triangular girth of the mast and, as I picked my way over it, three signs bolted on to the iron work came into view.

Danger Radiation

Danger High Voltage

NO UNAUTHORISED ASCENT

The overwhelming feeling was of displacement. 'What in God's name am I doing here?' But then I was past the warnings and ducking between the girders, already thirty feet above the ground and climbing on to the first triangular metal platform. Inside the steelwork it was darker, and I knew that I was well hidden from any onlookers. Below me Kyle was walking gently over the stones, Dan was already easing his way over the ring of barbed wire and I knew that he too would be reading the signs.

Alone on the first deck I took time to glance up the main ladder. No safety cage surrounded it. A hundred and fifty feet above I could see a section of the thin iron rungs illuminated by the first set of red lights. Beyond that, through the platforms, more lights succeeded each other by a hundred and fifty feet to the top. I laid my hands on the first few steps of that ladder and, with the realisation that this stairway stretched unbroken for one thousand and fifty feet, I started to climb.

When engaged in such a task, on a constant energy adrenaline feed, the mind overloads with stimuli to such an extent that the body works as an automaton. It becomes easy to climb, and once a rhythm is established the climber slips into a kind of overdrive. Through the rungs passing in front of my face tiny lights twinkled far out on the plain where people were sleeping. When I reached the next platform and squeezed through the triangular opening, I could feel the ironwork scraping down the backpack of my parachute. I shuddered to think what might happen if the closing pin was pushed out and the chute fell open inside the structure, for already a stiff breeze was beginning to blow.

Standing up straight at two hundred feet, I shook my arms and legs to loosen the muscles and saw that out in the

Watching a friend leave the
house in Islington, 260 feet
above the street

Shakespeare Tower seen from
Cromwell Tower – one hour
after taking this photograph I
stepped over the rail in centre
picture (*right*)

The entrance to Shakespeare
Tower – my landing zone

Groundrush over Houston in the bright Texan
sunshine (picture supplied by Photo-chuting Enterprises)

fields the light was growing. Below me the compound lights looked close and bright, but the general sounds all seemed far away, drowned out by the windrush. Presently my companions joined me and after a minute or two we continued, with Kyle setting the pace. Later, at the six-hundred-foot platform, I looked down through the opening to be greeted by the eerie sight of two red hands in the shadows climbing the ladder after me.

At seven hundred feet the structure became a more closed in affair as we started to ascend through the area of the transmitter itself. We climbed further, to where the ladder changed and was smaller and harder to grip with frozen dew-soaked gloves. There were no rest platforms now and we climbed the straight three hundred feet to the top. It was almost daylight, and we reckoned the wind to have strengthened to about forty miles an hour.

At one thousand and fifty feet the ladder disappeared through a square trapdoor in a triangular iron catwalk. I took hold of the handle and pushed it upwards. Squeezing through the opening and placing the trap down, I stepped off the ladder. Kyle and Dan joined me and we closed the trapdoor behind us. The feeling at that moment was a combination of intense emotions. A barely controlled fear, like boiling milk kept just in check, but ready to leap over into chaos, mingled with a sense of pride and a stark realisation of finality. The climb was over and we were at the edge. To climb down was unthinkable, to stay impossible. The spring was wound and the potential energy of fate strained against the safety catch of our courage.

Far below, crouching on the ladder with limbs not made for it, his black leather wings bound by the iron girders of the pylon, the carrion man angled his sightless head upward. Sniffing at the rungs, he croaked greedily, and spurred on by his hunger, he shuffled up the ladder toward us.

In the dictionary the word flight is defined as an act of escape as well as one of aviation. A thousand feet above the plain we prepared to do both. The chutes had been carefully packed and double-checked the night before, and we saw to it that each of our harnesses was properly fitted. It was bitterly cold to stand up there after our long exertion, and in the strengthening light we knew that the time to leave was upon us.

*

At a quarter past five Kyle removed his gloves and, with a final check, prepared to exit the platform. Around the edge there stood a rail at waist height. In each corner a red beacon, pale now in the early daylight, blinked on and off. Kyle folded his pilot chute – flapping and billowing in the strong wind – into his right hand and climbed over the barrier so that he was standing on the central bar and leaning back against the top rail. Dan watched through the camera to his right. From where I stood on the left, I could see Kyle's face, tense with excitement, as he stood looking straight down the thousand feet of girders that dropped away sheer beneath his feet.

Without another word he leaned forward fractionally and sprang away from us. It was a heart-stopping moment. For a split second he was frozen in upward flight and then he was gone, accelerating smoothly away down the tower. To us, he grew smaller and smaller, gaining more speed as he went. Then about three seconds off, the pilot chute went wide away from him to his right. Lazily it reached the end of the bridle line attaching it to the main canopy. And as Kyle sped ever faster towards the flat top of the compound buildings far below, the pilot inflated, bursting the backpack open and dragging out the main chute. Almost lost in the roar of the wind, we heard a faint crash as the big main canopy opened. Perfectly on heading, it flew the tiny figure quickly downwind away from the menacing structure.

Dan went next, and his jump was also perfect. A three-second freefall took him a hundred and fifty feet down the mast, and through sixty miles an hour from a standing start. The thought occurred to me that people will pay thousands of pounds for the fastest type of motor car and it will take twice as long to achieve that speed. As the light grew to full day I stowed the camera away inside my jacket and clambered over the rail.

It was strange to stand up there in the wind and the cold on the brink of the iron work. I cast a glance over my shoulder at the now empty metal triangle. No one knew that we were here, and when I left, as I would at any second, the cold steel platform would be deserted once more. I wondered how long it would be until another soul climbed the long stair and emerged through the trap. There was no reason for anyone to do so, the radio dishes on the top had been long since removed.

I looked forward down the stretch of the mast and then beyond to the tiny cottages and roadways out on the plain. Further down, individual antennae, some of them ten-feet long, stood out from the girders at intervals. Thousand-foot steel hawsers dropped away from colossal couplings to concrete staples far out in the surrounding fields where Kyle was just landing. It was time to go. I raised my arms and stood balancing on the rail, breathing deeply. The singing in my head reached a crescendo.

*

If I had listened then to the sounds beneath the howling wind, if I had been attuned enough to feel beyond the biting cold, I might have felt the hand that fell upon my shoulder. But we had no common language, the carrion man and I. His hand could not harm me. His touch fell on empty air, and without casting another glance behind, I kicked off into flight.

Physically, the still-air exit means that you fall away into a void, unlike the airflow that cushions you when jumping from a plane. There is silence as you begin to drop towards the ground. Then, after a couple of seconds, you hear the air start to move past. Your hair moves back from your face and the rushing sound begins to pick up. Your clothes press against your body. At this point on a jump from a fixed object you start to see the structure itself pick up speed.

When you leave an aeroplane, the ground seems a long way off. Even ten or fifteen seconds from impact, when normally you are opening your parachute, you don't really get an impression of the speed at which the ground is approaching. Some jumpers have experienced what is known as groundrush. This is not a healthy sign. Groundrush means that instead of seeing all the land spread out below, you fine-focus only a small area, usually your impact zone, and the rest is a blur. When standing in the middle of your living-room, looking at the carpet you can see a large area around your feet and the rest of the room in your peripheral vision; but lie down on your stomach with your nose a few inches from the floor and look straight down – that is the effect of groundrush. At under one thousand feet it can become apparent. In conventional freefall, and travelling at very high speed, this could mean that you have just over five seconds left to live.

When jumping from a pylon or cliff, the groundrush is instantaneous. You jump off, look down, and it feels at once as if impact is imminent. It is an illusion. Because any object falls slowly at first and then accelerates toward its terminal velocity, you can afford to wait a few seconds while the hard ground – appearing so close that only the impact zone is visible – comes rushing up at you. The ground just keeps coming and coming and after a few moments, when you are starting to enter the real acceleration phase, then you throw out your pilot chute and cheat the devil.

Here at the pylon groundrush is enhanced, for as the roofs of the buildings come zooming up to smash you, the girders of the structure start to blur as they measure your speed. The experience is as frightening as it is euphoric.

Seized by a violent and irresistible acceleration, I began the familiar pattern. Building and building, the momentum of madness pushed me towards the concrete. I know how this goes – I launch, I throw the pilot, I wait, I look down, I say 'Oh God', and then my canopy opens. I am breathless, my heart is pounding and my spirit failing as courage burns away like a tiny speck of phosphorus inside me.

I looked between my feet at the tower moving past.

The girders were flickering like passing sleepers in a railway track. Everything suddenly turned red as I passed the first set of lights. *Red?* Danger! Blood! Ruin! Straight down in the corn I could see last night's footprints leading to the fence. Further out there were flattened areas, driven into sleep-crazed patterns by the night.

A yearning pulled at my fingers. Pitch the pilot! Just *throw* it! But something, some mental terror clock inside me, kept my hand closed around the flapping fabric, denying control to fear. I could feel my jeans pressing on my shins. My toes in my shoes. It was three seconds since I had left the rail. Now the alarm bells rang out and, throwing the pilot chute as far away as I could, I looked down again. There was the sound of the chamber revolving just before the hammer falls in a game of Russian roulette, and bang! My canopy burst open.

A moment later I touched down beside Kyle and Dan on the soft grass of a beautiful spring morning. Exhilarated, we turned to make our way to the car, chattering so excitedly that we hardly heard the long drawn wail from high overhead. A tortured moan drifted down to us. No matter, only the wind in the girders, the air moving between the iron work and an angel of madness crying in hunger.

9

Night Creatures

If a leopard passes your door
            at some secret dead hour,
Pauses for an instant to sniff the threshold,
            And then walks on into the dark,
You will find his tracks in the morning
            still fresh on the ground,
And you'll know that something very beautiful,
                 but deadly,
has come far too close for comfort
            undercover of the night.

In my wonder I am drawn to you
            and in my fear I wish you gone.
Back along the path into the darkness.
And I'll sleep behind a locked door
              as I've always done.

So it was for the rest of that summer that a clan of us assumed a midnight brotherhood – pylon people, who came alive when others slept, stealing away in the dark and the cold and returning an hour after dawn. We were night creatures, going about our clandestine rendezvous and climbing the midnight ladder to the stars. Home to us was a tiny iron triangle in the sky. Watching a jumper from above was like seeing a man running down a darkened corridor past lit windows, a strobe illuminating him momentarily, reducing him in size with each beat until the parachute cracked open far beneath us.

Sometimes we would jump when the mast was in total cloud and no ground could be seen. The iron work stretched down to disappear in the soft white marshmallow sky while the black guy wires probed eerily away into the mist. On these occasions one felt the awful illusion that the platform might be ten or twenty thousand feet up. Always the pylon imparted to us a sense of belonging. We would take first-time jumpers to climb it and every time they would return home invigorated, having seen, felt and shared an experience beyond description.

Towards the end of summer we had people climbing the ladder, jumping down in the darkness, repacking their chutes in the field below and climbing back up to jump again at dawn. Countless leaps were made from the pylon without incident. No emergency chutes (a realistic possibility on so high an object) were used. Some jumps were made with two men linked together in freefall. Others opened their parachutes and linked them to make stack formations.

At the mast it was an eleven-second interval from

leaving the iron rail at a thousand feet to impacting on the tarmac below, should the chute fail to open. Compared to our five seconds at Cheddar Gorge, it was child's play, with ample time to use a reserve in an emergency. The site became so safe that the pylon people became a known underground movement at the airfield drop zone. Timings were arranged by word of mouth during the day so that one group visiting the mast would not bump into another, though this did happen from time to time.

On one occasion a group of four of us were at the four-hundred-foot platform when a car pulled into the compound below. It was two in the morning, and we knew that this could only be some kind of security patrol. There was no reason for anyone else to be there. Other jumpers would have parked near our vehicle which was hidden under the trees beyond the factory. Nervously we flattened ourselves against the girders. Suddenly one of the group, Crazy Larry, whispered 'Someone's coming up!'

'What?' I couldn't believe it.

'Someone is climbing the ladder,' Larry repeated.

'Oh, shit!'

I thought over the options. We could race to the top and try to get everyone over the rail before they got to us. Rushing a BASE jump is not a good idea, and doubly bad at night. The positive side was that if we flew off in four different directions and met back at the car the odds of capture were slight. I looked down through the girders. There on the stretch of ladder directly below our platform, a pair of hands, detached and lit red by the beacons on the mast, were padding up the rungs towards us.

We waited, wondering what to do. To my mind there

was no way that a policeman was going to climb up here in the middle of the night. They would not be crazy enough. Maintenance crew use harnesses and stay attached to the structure by cables. I could hear no sound of such equipment. There was an aura of intrusion and secrecy in their movement. Suddenly the hands below stopped climbing. For a second all was still. Then a face appeared like a materialising ghost as the climber looked up. We four stood silent, peering down at him fifteen feet below. I figured that if he were unfriendly he would have said something, so I whispered as loudly as I dared –

'C'mon, it's okay. Come up.'

Two of them climbed the last few feet and emerged through the trap. They were jumpers from the airfield whom we knew. That made six of us. Giggling like children, we waited for the patrol car to leave and then continued on to the top. By two-thirty, all six of us had jumped and disappeared into the night.

*

Psychologists in New York have noted an alarming trend among some police officers who believe that the wearing of a firearm on one's hip is the same as using it. The more often the cop draws his weapon and gets the desired effect without having discharged any rounds, the more likely he is to feel secure in a tight situation. The result may be that, on a given night, he will find himself on the wrong side of the line separating acceptable risk from extreme danger. Without back-up and outnumbered, he might quickly find himself short on both rounds and courage.

Just as a person's body can suffer injury, so can their spirit, and it can be temporary or permanent. Spiritual injury can leave a scar just as ragged as any on the living flesh, and while bullets, or parachutes, can save your body from harm, only courage can save your spirit. If courage fails you at the moment of truth, though time will heal the wound, you may carry the spirit scar to your grave.

Spirit death is the most fearsome prospect. We are prey to the knowledge that, when our time comes to walk into the dark – even though the call might come from within – we could be found wanting and run screaming like children, scared that we may glimpse there the sinewy heel of some towering, hidden doom. Courage fails when that knowledge gains the upper hand. The more times we win without firing a shot, or without using a reserve chute, the more confident we become. Better to face live combat experience which, in any form, brings the ego crashing down.

*

When winter set in it became too cold to climb the mast. The steel rungs of the ladder were covered with ice and the bitterness of the night wind took all the spirit from even the most courageous among us. Daylight came late, and by the time the jumper had enough vision to make his leap the factory below was buzzing with activity.

In London, my friend Larry asked if I would go with him to reconnoitre a building, with a view to jumping from the top floor. It was a twenty-three-storey building – only two hundred and seventeen feet high – which would afford no more than three and a half seconds to impact.

We met in a bar with our chutes already packed and headed for the building where we found the landing zone more than a little crowded. It was a triangle of grass about a hundred feet along its base and stretching away to an apex two hundred feet from the building. On this lawn stood a scattering of stone benches, a concrete walled fountain and several trees and shrubs. I reckoned on being under canopy for maybe six seconds, and with all these obstacles – together with the surrounding spiked iron fence – I was somewhat dubious.

Apart from Steve at Cheddar, BASE jumpers who injured themselves usually did so on landing. I had seen perfect jumps with immaculate openings spoiled by the jumper missing the landing zone, or crashing hard into the ground due to a short canopy ride in light wind conditions. Often this resulted in no more than a fast rollover in the mud and bruised pride, though sometimes jumpers would hurt an ankle or wrist, or even break a bone.

'It's kinda tight,' I said, understating my thought.

'Yeah, but you know we're not going far from that height' – Larry held up his foot – 'and we only need this much room to land.'

'Well, it's not so much the distance you travel as the time you've got to get your act together.' I felt confident that we could safely make the jump but the risk factor seemed unnecessarily high.

We thought of landing in the street, and sat for some time counting the seconds between cars. Eight was a good average, but as the exit point was over a balcony on the top floor, facing one way down the street, it would be a matter of luck if a car appeared from behind the block as you got under canopy.

'Come on, let's go up and have a look,' said Larry.

Slowly the lift rattled upwards. Graffiti was scrawled
on the walls and the floor was rank with urine. When
the door clattered open, we walked to the balcony and
looked out over London. It felt really high. The swing
door two hundred feet below creaked open, the sound
echoing up to us, and we saw someone walk across the
grass. *Groundrush.*

It was windy at the top, a steady breeze gusting so that
we squinted into it. It was blowing directly into the face
of the building, and we decided that a skydive was out of
the question. Too many things were wrong. There would
be other times. Jump platforms would not go away. We
turned and left silently, passing the doors of people's
dwellings, invisible to them, ghostly figures walking on
the landings, intruders.

The response we usually get if these people find us is:
'Who are you?' – followed by: 'I'm calling the police.'
However even the police are powerless to do much other
than tell us to leave, and we are going anyway. There is no
law which forbids us to jump from objects. All the same,
the thought of it happening is sufficiently threatening for
people to act as if there is, and to take steps to prevent us.
The police take us away and question us, but ultimately,
in the absence of a law written in black and white, they let
us go. Trespass is a tenuous charge. Breach of the peace,
unlawful display – none of them stands up to scrutiny.
None the less the two or three hours spent in a holding
cell while they pore over their books can be uncomfort-
able. For this reason BASE jumpers shy away from attention and prefer a trouble-free life in the shadows.

I can understand residents being afraid that we might
damage their properties or burgle them, but in fact, we do

less damage than the pigeons. There is nothing sinister about our calling. Yet even if they see what we are doing, even if we say it's all right and tell them we'll do no harm, still they want us to leave and threaten us.

Imagine that in a dream you walk out upon high places and fly from the roofs and clifftops, soar in the sky and land unharmed on tiptoe among your friends, laughing and happy. Nothing to pay. No more equipment than a tiny backpack weighing ten pounds or less. That was all we wanted – merely to celebrate our new-found wings. Fear was a long-dead spectre whose corpse rolled back from where we now stood. We thought the battle won, Pandora's box open to the sky and the harpie of chaos exiled to howl unheard. In the midst of our victory the demonseed cracked open and an unmet foe stepped into the arena. For there is a moment when probability and chance align and breathe new life into our worst fears. As we turned, picked up our gear and left, somewhere in the night another tumbler clicked into place.

*

The next afternoon I returned to the bar to pick up my equipment which I had left there for safekeeping. On leaving for the station, my curiosity was aroused by the sight of three tall black apartment blocks some half a mile away. It was the Barbican complex, visible between the nearer buildings. Outside the underground station I stopped to look once more, and having time on my hands, I turned and started walking towards them. From somewhere a half-remembered conversation drifted back to me. An American voice:

'Anybody ever jump off one of them?'

'Must have . . . '
'No, man – I mean parachute jump.'
'If they did then I've never heard of it.'

When I reached the first tower I was staggered by the size of it. Four hundred and twenty feet high, a man-made mountain of black masonry with the sharp corners of the balconies jutting out down one side like the vertebrae of some ancient dinosaur. The doors leading into the building were closely guarded by video monitors. These apartments in the very heart of the city are the province of millionaires and film stars. I was ready to turn and walk back to the station when I spotted a small discreet side door of wired glass. I stepped forward and turned the handle. To my amazement, the door opened silently inwards. I looked around me and passed quickly into the concrete stairwell of the fire escape. Behind me in the silence the door closed with a sharp echoing sound.

In his headlong dive the harpie passed through a thousand miles an hour with ease. The wind rushing into his face drew the cracked lips back revealing stained yellow fangs, pitted and streaked. The sightless eyes narrowed to fierce slits and the pitch leather membranes of his wings rippled and snapped with the speed . . .

10

With Sure Direction

The Barbican comprises a labyrinth of convention halls and exhibition rooms set among neatly walled gardens with a brick inlaid walkway. The main thoroughfare takes traffic from Farringdon through a four-lane tunnel which runs beneath the ground towards Old Street. This means that, once on the premises, pedestrian traffic takes the place of cars. The show pieces are the three towers, all more or less identical. Until the recent construction of Canary Wharf in the East India Docks, the central block, Shakespeare Tower, was the tallest residential building in Britain. The triangular towers stand in line from east to west so that, from the open-air underground station, one obscures the others. Each block has a helipad on the roof and a bright yellow line painted on the floor of the stairwell leads up to it. In the event of fire, one has only to 'follow the yellow brick road' through the smoke to evacuation and safety. Curiously though, the roof is only accessible with a key obtained at the desk thirty-nine storeys below and that key must be signed out.

In the circumstances, I doubted the deskman's willingness to surrender it to me. The only other way into the open air was via the viewing balconies of the privileged tenants. These were separate from the balconies of the actual apartments.

When I reached the top stair, the landing ended with a door identical to the one four hundred feet below. There was a notice telling me that this door was wired to an alarm in reception and that any attempt to open it and gain access to the balcony would alert the security patrol. On careful examination, however, I found that the door was not fully closed. Several which I had tried on the way up had been locked but, as luck would have it, this top floor exit was open a quarter of an inch. A wire attached to the door ran down the wall, and I supposed that, though the door was not open enough to trip the alarm, any attempt to open it wider would do so immediately. Dropping my gear down, I sat on the top stair to think.

Outside was full daylight, and if I leapt from the balcony my only escape would be on foot. To avoid capture, I might do better to wait until darkness fell. In my mind the coincidences linked together. The chance finding of an open door below on such a highly guarded building, my walking past with parachute specially packed for a building jump when I should have been working, the fact that the top door should have been alarmed yet was open when all the others had been locked – it all pricked at the nape of my neck.

I sat listening to the lift gear running alongside me in a secret chamber concealed within the walls. Through three long hours I sat and alternately decided to go ahead and then in the same instant felt the almost uncontrollable desire to run back down the stairs and flee. Every now and then a footstep on the public landing behind me sent me leaping down the steps to hide on the floor below, but no one entered the stairwell. Not a soul in the world knew I was there . . . save one.

The carrion man hovered on the draught of air that rose up the face of the building. His clawed hands flexed and then closed around the edge of the roof as he settled above the empty balcony. Folding his great black wings, he too waited for the darkness in which he always sought his prey.

Jumping on other occasions, I had blindly overlooked the moments when doubt pointed to the dangers. There had been the presence of my friends to strengthen me. Shared pride had assured me of courage then, but now I was answerable to no one, and my heart sank. Having brought myself to the edge and looked upon the dare, I found that all I wanted was to run. No part of me wanted to open the door and step over the rail. Yet everything in me yearned to feel that euphoric surge pounding through my body. Gradually I overcame my fear and moved into that unshakable state called 'purpose'. I turned away from the plentiful warnings and excuses that my brain offered.

Night was falling across the city and lights were coming on. I got up, walked across the landing and stood looking through the glass door at the opposite tower. Thirty-nine storeys all lit up orange, red and yellow. Far below lay the street, mapped out in bright headlamps, teeming with people and cars. The open-air underground station crackled and flashed blue sparks, and beyond, awesome with its output of power, London was twenty miles of lights.

I pulled on my chute and checked it. Time to go. Necessity decreed that I take all my possessions with me so that no trace was left of my passing. Symbolically I was like a fighter donning armour before entering the fray, for the layers of clothing were all that might protect me from the ravages of the harpie's embrace. At last I laid my hand on the cold steel door and focused on my own reflection in the glass. A face of desperate commitment gazed back at me. Disgusted with my loitering, I turned the handle and stepped out into the cold. Above me the harpie shot bolt upright and began to move excitedly from side to side along the roof's edge, gloating and slavering.

Somewhere a clock chimed five. Inside the building the alarm bells must be ringing, and I thought of the tiny lift containing the security guards that would even now be ascending towards me. There was no hurry, no doubt assailed me, I had nowhere to go but over the edge. Gripping the masonry, I clambered up on to the left hand side of the balcony until I was balancing on the thin rail with one hand on the wall for support. On the ground hundreds of people were milling around, the noise wafting upward. Opposite I could see into living-rooms level with me in the next block. Beyond that, the lights of London faded into the distance, and above all the stars sparkled frostily in the cold December night.

I took a final glance back at the empty balcony and its

yawning glass door. For hours there had been the hollow-
ness of the stairwell and the echoes for company. Now, in
the flat featureless night, I felt small and alone. Turning, I
leaned forward, looked straight down, and jumped. From
ten feet above me the carrion man also jumped landing
square on my back, and we fell away from the thirty-
ninth floor together. After looking out across the black
plain of London spattered with twinkling lights, the con-
trast of the scene below was a glaring madness rushing up
at me.

My fragmented focus took in the window on the next
floor silently passing, and the flicker of the rain drip
gutter, so close that I could see the cracked paint. Beneath
me the grey asphalt was marked out into the dotted lines
of parking bays, and looming into view came a white
painted 'Emergency Services Only'. Cradled in a cannon-
ball of flesh, my consciousness kept taking pictures as I
hurtled through the cold, clammy air. The chamber re-
volved, and ten feet out from the glass on the twenty-
ninth floor the hammer fell. My parachute crashed open
and I saw it flying clear, away from the building. But on
looking up, I finally saw the true face of my madness. As I
watched, the parachute turned through one hundred and
eighty degrees until it was facing the building less than ten
feet out and three hundred feet above the street. Three
storeys later the canopy hit the corner balcony, hung up,
collapsed, ripped through and dropped me. Gaining
acceleration, I tried to catch the balcony below as I fell
past. My arms smashed across it, numbing them both so
that I thought them broken. Then I was tumbling help-
lessly, smacking arms and legs against the stonework,
cartwheeling from floor to floor. Still in the harness of

my shredded parachute I fell for two hundred feet.

I held my crossed arms over my face and head, desperately hoping that I would not dash my skull open. I fell in a sitting position, smashing the base of my spine again and again on the stonework, and then bouncing down to the next ledge and banging a shoulder on it.

I remember looking up the column of lit balconies, and then smacking into another, looking down at the street lamps zooming up to me, and cringing and hunching my shoulders as I crashed to the next. The overall feeling was certainly not one of fear; there was no time for that. In my mind I was completely convinced that at any second my back, my neck, my skull, that everything would shatter on the ground and I would be dead. Realising that this was all there was, that I had lived my life, came as a shock. Plans for tomorrow, next week, whenever, none of it mattered because there was to be no more. It was as close to the moment, the 'now' beyond the one-thirtieth, as I had ever been. I am about to die, NOW.

The last time I had seen the street lamps they had looked really big. I knew that I was very low and that I had only moments left. Something within me that paid no heed to logic made me reach for my reserve. In truth there was no possible way the reserve chute would open or even get line stretch in time. But it was really the only thing left. Falling at speed, skittering down the face of the masonry, my eyes now tight shut and my back hunched in a futile attempt to survive the last impact, I hooked my thumb of my right hand into the reserve handle.

But before I had time to pull the handle, everything, all the madness and speed, came to a sudden stop.

On the thirteenth floor the shredded material that was

left of my canopy caught momentarily on the corner stone of the balcony. Smashed and bruised ten feet below I hung swinging against the next floor. With numbed and gory hands from which the skin had been ripped I grabbed the stone sill as the sound of tearing cloth reached me from above. A shadow engulfed me. I screamed out loud and then all was still.

I hung there with the edge of the balcony in front of my nose and my arms hooked over it. The last chance and the split second to use it had produced a response and a strength that I thought had gone from me. Looking down over my right shoulder, I could see cars moving to and fro, people still walking home. Not a soul had seen me. My mind having surrendered to and been fixed on the fact that I was about to die, I now had to summon back the instinct to survive, rather than just letting the ledge slip easily from my arms and falling away backwards the hundred feet or so to the road. I was aching and hurt. To give in would be so easy. Death from impact must be painless. How long does it take for the body and skull to crush on the ground and squeeze the ghost out of the living flesh? What kind of now was that? Too fast for pain, I was sure.

Fight. If we stay long enough on the threshold of the door between the dead and the dying we alienate ourselves from either. Fight. You are here, you are not dying. That has passed. Your choice is to live, but you must fight. You are living; your dying has stopped. Now is not your time. Now is life. Now is LIFE!

With a desperate surge I put all my remaining spirit into a frantic kick and hooked my right foot on to the ledge. I pulled myself up to lie across the foot-wide balcony wall with my ribs aching and my heart pounding. I stopped for a second with my head facing outward and looked down again to the street. Christ! It looked as if it would suck me in, could just pull me clean off the wall, like at Clifton Bridge.

I eased myself down inside the balcony and slumped to my hands and knees on plush matting. The rigging lines of my parachute hung from the balcony above so that it looked as if I were caught in a spider's web. Now, for the first time, I peered into the apartment on whose balcony I had landed. There were potted plants everywhere, a black leather sofa and a glass coffee table, complete with steaming coffee cups. A television set danced colours at me through a big picture window, and in the kitchen I could see the shadow of somebody making dinner.

Now the instinct to fight rather than surrender was replaced by the need to flee. Senselessly the urge to run charged me with energy, not prompted by anything more than an impulse to distance myself from the whole thing. I guess that it was a conditioned reflex. As soon as you land, disappear. The normal reason is to avoid arrest and incurring the wrath of the powers that be; now I merely wanted to go, to get out.

I tried for a minute to pull the parachute down from the upstairs balcony, but it was stuck fast and so irreparably ripped that I hit the single point release pad and shrugged it off my shoulders. On the left of the balcony a narrow corridor, maybe three-feet wide, branched off to the apartment's fire escape. Fending myself off the plate glass window with bloodied hands, I lurched down this escape route and crashed into the fire door. Grimacing with pain, I felt for the bar handle in the dim light and threw myself bodily against it. The door clicked open and I fell into the twelfth-floor landing, barely keeping on my feet. Opposite the lift doors with their ornamental number panels was the main stairwell. Reeling across the landing, I hurtled down the stairs to escape.

In my flight I never for an instant stopped to reason out any course of action. All I knew was that I had to get away. Pounding down the last few steps, I crashed through one door after another, expecting at any moment to find security staff blocking my escape. Even as I emerged from the glass door that I had entered so long ago I felt as if they were hurrying to intercept me. I walked away, not running, just walking as fast as I could into the shadows. And half-way across the floodlit landing site my nerve broke and I ran into the night. I turned right and moved through the crowds on the street. Above me the ragged strip of my canopy shifted slightly in the breeze way up on the thirteenth floor. I stopped in a shop doorway and looked at myself in the glass. White and slack-jawed, my reflection stared back at me, blood on the nose running along the lip to the chin. Then the aching started to come in waves from within.

People walking past looked at me and then away. I was a blank, some guy with nothing better in his life to do than bang about in shop doorways at night. Don't talk to him, he's either crazy or dangerous. Looks as if he's had a fight already. Come on.

As I walked off into the night waves of pain washed over me from my lower back, the raw flesh on my hands and elbows stinging. Every joint ached. I was shaking uncontrollably and limping badly now. My throat felt tight, choking me with emotion. My ribs ached terribly when I breathed. Eventually I stopped at a dingy bar and sat shaking in the corner while alcohol eased my state of shock.

After some time I took a night bus to north London where my brother rented an apartment. Nobody answered when I knocked. Pale and shaking, still in shock, I pulled up the tarpaulin on the back of his pick-up truck and eased my way inside to sleep on the bare metal floor. I pulled the tarpaulin back over me, shutting out the night and the December cold as best I could. The moon crept across the cover and over the shape curled beneath it.

I I

Dare and Be Damned

Sobbing in benighted cells,
   Lifers who never knew their crime,
   Toll the bell for a fallen hero.
   Midnight hears a single chime,
      Screams for pity echo in the city –
   I only did it once . . . until the next time.

To justify a moment's existence, however fleeting, demands the simple statement – I am. This is wilful risk-taking, encountering danger and therefore experiencing fear. Curiosity may drive the seeker to examine whether there is a point beyond which he will not progress. The end result is a mental version of Darwin's natural selection. It is spiritual evolution at work. Just as this bad spirit which I call the harpie may be starved into

106

submission, so also may he be the victim of his own gluttony.

It took several days for the injuries I sustained to heal, but the scars were deepest on my spirit. That which I had witnessed in others had come suddenly to me. It was as if some ancient shaman had applied his leeches and drawn out the bad blood. For the blood of madness possessed those outings as surely as it did any lunatic who screamed through the barred windows at the awful silver moonlight.

For a time I was cured, yet though it might be deemed a salvation, I felt lessened by it. Doubting myself, ever and again the question would rise up in me, sense or cowardice? At night a mocking laughter haunted the darker corners. Morning, I fancied, brought deep gouges to the window sill and, now and again, a single black feather on the grass below.

While meditating with the room darkened but for candlelight, and with incense burning, I fought this strange new malady. For now there hung upon my spirit a listless fever. I had tasted something of which I once dreamed. Not just the physical joy of street flight but the pounding immediacy of the spirit statement. I fought back the doubt that mocked my courage and each night pondered the wisdom of taking up the gauntlet. I came to see accident as the simple alignment of ill fortune which was unpredictable once the environment of danger was entered. Indeed wherever accident might mean death, the engagement now seemed to be one of ritual suicide. The relationship I had formed with risk and fear seemed to have become a childish game in the face of this realisation. Just like the spin of the five hundredth coin, the odds of each jump being successful were still fifty/fifty. Would it open all right or wouldn't it? All else was trivial.

Something in me wanted to go again, for just as at Cheddar there was a score to settle. The notion excited me but the reality was too awful to contemplate. When the coin had dropped, my name had been on it, and this time it had nearly been the end. Sense told me that enough was enough, and yet to finish on so disastrous an outing did not seem right. It was as though a challenge was before me. My worst fears had come true and by incredible good fortune I had survived that meeting. But if I let it stop me I would never know if I had been living a false dream.

Over the next two weeks my body healed. The physical damage had been superficial, but my spirit bled, and would not stop. Eventually I took up the gauntlet once more and packed my chute for one last attempt.

Alone in a crowded tube train, with my new canopy in a sack at my feet, I rode the underground. You may have been in the same carriage that night and seen the blank dressed in black, going grim-faced downtown. As the train pulled into Barbican station I shaded the glare of internal lighting from the window and squinted into the dark. I caught a brief glimpse of the nearest column of lights, stark against the night. Walking through the barrier, I left the station and there it was, towering into the starlight like the gaunt unscalable pillars of some ancient henge.

The raised area surrounding the whole Barbican complex is called the podium level. It is a maze of covered walkways and passages. The inhabitants are suited and gloved and stride authoritatively. Beneath the podium, whose discreet doors giving into the towers are locked and safe, the main entrance hall stands open but brightly lit, guarded by watchmen behind broad desks, braided uniforms lending them arrogance and aggression. In later years we learned to call the bluff of such self-importance by dressing as natives and boldly answering their intimidation at the London Hilton. But at this time the legacy of Mendlesham and her ninja tactics were more the norm. Darkly dressed in loose fatigues and soft shoes, and carrying a dark canvas bag in black leather hands, I advanced through the shadows, keeping well to the side away from the lighting.

Going to each tower in turn I laid my hand excitedly on the door catch and pushed, all the time watching for unwanted attention as I visited each fire door and was met by disappointment. The concrete stairwell visible through the glass tantalised me. Looking up at the tower from which I had jumped, I stood on the very spot where my corpse would have lain had fortune not saved me. Counting the floors my gaze fell upon the corner apartment of the twelfth. The lights were on and a shadow crossed the ceiling of the balcony. He was at home, but he did not know that his unwanted visitor had returned. Could I ever tell him why? Would he think me crazy? Was I indeed going beyond reason now?

I turned to walk further, hoping to find another entrance which might yield to me. Two figures were advancing down the passageway from the podium and in an involuntary burst of movement we three recoiled from each other. I half turned back to the locked door, patting my pockets as if to find my imaginary key. They quickly stepped back out of the passage and into the main garden area. Then we all froze for a second and looked more closely at each other's silhouettes.

'Kyle?' I asked.

'I don't believe it!' came the reply. I hoisted my gearbag on to my shoulder and walked toward them, laughing.

'Bloody hell! Is that you two?'

'You fucking maniac, what are you doing here?'

As I have said, like attracts like, and with a limited number of objects from which to jump, I and my Mendlesham friends had been drawn to the same place. Together we continued the search but to no avail. So like the desperate conspirators we were, we withdrew into the shadows to wait. Now and then an elegant figure would appear on the podium sheathing his gold-ringed hands with warm gloves and buttoning a three-quarter length mohair coat. As soon as they were far enough away one of us would bound through the darkness to try the door which had been left to swing shut.

Sometimes a policeman would come patrolling through the gardens with their twinkling fountains and ornate lamps. We would watch him from behind the honeycomb masonry, silent and breathless. Eventually we gave up, it was not the time. It was around midnight when we melted away into the streets and returned home.

Up on the twelfth floor the light had been turned out an hour since and the occupants lay long asleep.

*

As it turned out I was not to meet the challenge for some time. After that first luckless visit the door had closed, and though I returned several times throughout the winter, the lock stayed firmly in place. Kyle and Dan did eventually manage to sneak in and make successful jumps, but that was a long time afterwards. For my part, I took to going out a couple of nights each week by train into the more built-up suburbs. There I would take visual bearings on the first tall building I saw and walk the streets until I found my way to the foot of it. During that period I must have walked many miles in pursuit of my imagined holy grail. Once at the building I used to wait in cover until a resident approached with his key, whereupon I would fall in alongside him and gain entry.

Don't let anyone tell you that the ghettos of Los Angeles or New York are any tougher than those of east London. For there I visited places in which I genuinely feared for my safety, though I am not a small person and have known my share of bar-room brawls. There were times when I would stand in the squalid lift of some run down building, waiting for the door to open on the top landing, and steel myself for confrontation. I came across burnt out apartments where squatters still lived with their possessions laid out in the charred and blackened rooms. Burst refuse sacks, piled up beside rubbish chutes which had been blocked for years, spilled stinking garbage in graffiti-daubed corridors. Rotting mattresses lay in the darker corners where alcoholics and drug addicts would bed down for the night.

Often I found myself both appalled and saddened by the children playing in these rat-infested slums – children whose futures seemed every bit as dim as their current existence. In some buildings the lifts would not be working, and here old people who could no longer leave their apartments depended on friends to bring them groceries. I came to think that even some people with a roof over their heads in London qualified as homeless. It may have been only a few miles to the Barbican, but socially it was another continent.

Soon I was able to locate the fire escape door within seconds of setting foot on the top landing of any building. In all the tower blocks from Southwark Park to Wandsworth, or from Islington to Battersea, the one common ground was this no-man's-land – left out of the lift to the end of the hallway, through a heavy fire-check door and suddenly there would be nothing but echoes and bare concrete. Then up and up, breathless and sweating, to the final barrier of the roof door, which was invariably locked. Children playing love to throw things from rooftops, and though I wanted only to throw myself, I too found the way barred.

Sometimes I would stumble around in the Stygian darkness of a utility room, stepping over hurdles of pipework with my hands outstretched before me, and with dust and pigeon dirt thick underfoot. Once, in a building in Vauxhall, I found a roof door made of widely spaced thick steel bars between which I could easily fit my leg. I was able to place my foot on the rooftop but that was all, and though I rattled the gate with all my strength, in the mocking silence that fell I could not pass. The moonlight shone on pools of rainwater out on the asphalt, and twenty feet away a perfect exit point two hundred feet above the road tormented me. I pushed my arms through the bars then and hung there, thinking of my friends at home. Not for the last time I wondered what I was doing.

My disappointment thinly masked the fear which I knew would come clamouring out of the night on the occasion when all the doors opened for me again. I could not unlearn what I had come to know, and where once a tiny voice had whispered poison to my dream, now it jabbered with the certain authority of doom. Adrenaline addiction is exquisite, but the risk is of an infection both incurable and deadly.

12

The Gauntlet

Crazy Larry is driving the white Volkswagen and we are oozing paranoia as we sit at the lights in City Road. The music was turned off a mile back, when the house first came into view. The house is twenty-six storeys high and showing now all the time above the nearer blocks blasting out light that fades the further it gets so that the building is bathed in a greenish halo. It looks as if the night is a painted sheet and someone has added the building before the rest was dry, so that it is blurred around the edges.

In the elevator we stand in silence and listen to invisible people in their far-off cells, eating and banging cutlery. They talk with loud bouncing echoes of gossip, inciting us with scandal as we pass secretly upwards inside the wall.

'Ascending to a higher plain,' I say with mock sincerity.

'Descending to a higher plain,' Larry replies, tapping the bag containing our chutes. The lift jolts to a halt and the door sighs open.

'How about, transcending a higher *plane?*'

We laugh briefly and quickly stifle the sound as we walk out into a corridor full of night air.

The noise of traffic is far off as we walk directly to the balcony. A mile across a glittering sea of light, the G.P.O. tower is twice as tall as us, blasted against the darkness like a beacon. It reminds me of one of those toadstools which call flies with irresistible messages, only to trap them with acid enzymes secreted from glands of treachery. At the highest point the red lights shout danger, but the attraction of that subtle calling draws us onward.

I like the notion that each apartment holds a story which fragments and interconnects beyond its walls, in the same way that cars and taxi-cabs bear the millions to their rendezvous. This is the invisible theme to which all major cities dance and vibrate. This is the pulse of life, the chain reaction whereby all civilisation sprawls under the darkening sky.

*

The door to the roof is locked and the only way that we can gain access is to climb up on to the twenty-sixth balcony and pull ourselves up between the overhanging roof beams. The prospect is daunting. To jump off is to exercise control, but to fall off would be catastrophic. Larry goes up first and I hoist the bag on to my shoulder. He leans back through the concrete girders and pulls it silently up behind him. Ignoring the panic which is babbling in my brain, I hurry myself into action. A grip on

115

the wall, a hand on the rail, and I vault up with both knees on the edge. Now balance makes me lean forward and suddenly I am looking straight down the two-hundred-and-fifty-foot edifice. Shakily I stand and, reaching overhead, grip the overhang. The rest is an easy swing up, and I am through.

Once we are on the roof itself the pressure is eased a little. Now we have penetrated like thieves into the throne room and the charade of our secrecy is done. Out of the risk of detection, we have all the time in the world to prepare.

'Right now, Larry, let's just take in the scenery for a minute,' I say, pushing back my sleeves.

'Yeah,' he replies. 'What do you think?' He's asking about the conditions.

'No problem,' I tell him.

'There's a little breeze you know. Let's get it right.'

'Breeze is nothing.' I am standing on the corner, looking out, talking over my shoulder at him.

Larry comes over next to me and pulls a piece of tissue out of his pocket. He throws it forward and it blows straight back into his face, but it is no more than a breath and the tissue doesn't weigh a thing.

'It's incoming,' he says.

'It's nothing.'

'Right, okay. No hurry.' He is talking to himself now. 'Let's just take our time.'

'Yeah, we have the rest of our lives to think about it.'

I didn't mean to spook him with that one. It was bravado for my own good.

The roof is flat with a foot-high wall all around it. Four feet back from the edge there is a rail at waist height. In the centre of the roof is the lift motor room which has a long sloping top that comes down to within a yard of the floor. We have been up here for about ten minutes and now it is obvious that the jump is on. Larry drags his kit, jingling and clanking, out of the bag and checks it. I'm rigging static lines to the rail to assist the deployment of our chutes. Everything seems to be going to plan . . .

Suddenly I become aware that we are not alone. I turn, not knowing why. No sound has reached me, no flicker of movement, and yet there, right behind me, visible below the overhang of the lift motor room, I can see somebody's legs. Snatching up the heavy canvas bag I whisper urgently.

'There's someone up here!'

'What?'

'Come on!'

The intruder is almost at the corner of the lift room. Another second and he will be upon us. We scamper away to the lee side of the motor house and find a doorway in which to hide. Inside is a braillescape of machinery, cables and wheels. Danger signals alert me against making contact with anything which might move suddenly, snagging a hand or sleeve and dragging me into the lift mechanism. I put the bag down and whisper Larry to be still. At that moment someone steps into the doorway and looks in at us.

In the dim light on the roof I am face to face with the biggest man I've ever seen. For a second we stand in front of each other with only the door frame between us. If we wanted, we could reach out and shake hands, we are that close. But three feet away from his eyes I am invisible. He knows that something is there but he's damned if he's crossing the threshold to find out what. From inside, where the illusion of nothingness makes it seem as if that seven-by-three doorway is all there is, he stands with the whole world behind him.

For a long moment we stare at each other, him uncertain, head turning very slightly this way and that. Then Larry moves, invisibly. The leg strap buckle of his chute clangs against a metal locker. The guy jumps like he's touched a live wire, and then turns to get away. In a shot I have realised that he too is an intruder. Whispering Larry to stay put, I am through the door and after him.

'Hey! Hey you, wait a minute.'

He stops at the corner of the motor room and half turns. Then I see his two buddies come out of the shadows. Neither of them is as big but both are broad and swarthy, Latin-looking fellas.

'What are you doing up here?' I try to put authority in my voice but know that I am on thin ice.

'Nothin', man,' says the big one. 'Just lookin' around, you know.'

'You the caretaker or something?' I ask, knowing that he is not. There is no reply, so I walk up to him and try a smile.

'It's okay, nothing's wrong. Me and my pal in there are workmen, just dropping off some tools, that's all.'

He knows that I am lying, but I figure it's a good time to let him know there're two of us.

'Workmen huh.' It's a statement. It tells me that he wants more and knowing that he has no right to be here either I let him hear it.

'Well, no, that's not exactly true. To be honest, I'm up

here taking pictures. You just spooked me a little.' The tension eases and I push them further.

'So what are you here for?' Silence. 'It's all right, man. I'm not the law. I shouldn't be here either.'

That does the trick. The smallest man steps forward out of the shadow and I realise that he is the leader. He looks Italian, with sharp clothes, flat face and in the full moonlight thick jet black eyebrows which meet over the bridge of his nose.

'We're pirates.'

'You're *what*?' I say, laughing.

'Radio pirates. We've been looking for a place to put up a transmitter.'

'No shit?'

I admit I'm taken aback. Though it sounds fair enough. While we talk I begin to test the static lines, picking them up out of the shadows where they are hanging down from the rail. They see this and gather around in a group. By the same instinct with which I knew them, they know me.

'What are you doing, man?' They make no bones about seeing straight through my workmen, photographer spiel. I let go of the rope and lean against the rail with both elbows.

'You want to put a mast on it, I want to parachute off it. Don't tell on me and I won't tell on you.'

There is a little ripple of laughter. When they see that I am not smiling their manner changes from disbelief to wonder. I drop the lines down and walk to the doorway. Larry, who has heard everything, steps out into the light and I pull the kit bag from behind the locker. We return to the group as they stand in silence, shuffling around and exchanging glances. Then someone sees that Crazy Larry is wearing his parachute.

'Christ! He means it,' mutters the Italian.

They stand and watch as we prepare to jump. We put on our helmets and make constant equipment checks. Our talk is probably a little strange to them.

'Risers clear?'

'Yeah, they're fine. Static is tied and the line is clear.'

'Leg straps are equal and the cutaway is taped off.'

'Mind you don't tread on the line.'

'Would you check my break tie.'

'You got once round and tied off well. It's clear and the routing is correct.'

The normal banalities which every skydiver has heard a million times make them laugh and start to joke. Fearing that somebody on the top balcony might overhear them, I send the group over to the other side of the roof. They will get a better view from there. I tell them not to forget what they are about to see and they assure me that they won't.

The lines are tied off and we now enter the part of the jump with which I am familiar but still not used to – waiting for the moment. Larry is to go first, and I'll follow him. The landing zone is a big well-lit concrete building plot opposite. The conditions are perfect. I look at Larry. He is standing well back from the edge, his fingers clenching and relaxing about twice a second. He is jigging from one foot to the other and looking straight out like if he doesn't look down over the edge it won't hurt him. I glance in that direction and see that he is staring at the G.P.O. tower, glittering away on the skyline. Holding the static line clear of his feet I tell him quietly, 'Okay you're checked and clear. You can go any time you like now.'

Without looking at me, still staring straight ahead, he says, 'Right . . . See you down there.'

Then he steps up on to the wall, spreads his arms to embrace the emptiness and steps calmly off the roof of the building. The only sound as he falls past the top floor window is the hiss of the static line snaking over the edge after him. I stand breathless and watch Larry drop away from me, dark against the street below. His hands are spread, palms down, head craning skyward almost Christ-like. The line whiplashes back as it breaks away from the attachment point and Larry's parachute, so close that I could step off the roof and walk on it, wallows forward into the night. He releases the brakes and the canopy surges forward into full drive. Then he is out over the street, circling round to the right and sighting on the landing zone.

As I watch him guide his flying machine down across the crowded road and between the lamp posts to the ground it seems like the most beautiful and fulfilling thing in the world. All the more so because of our audience – not for the sake of showing off, but of sharing. Larry lands, his body is invisible, though I can see the solid appearance of the nylon parachute fabric shake once and then crumple into a shapeless blur. A whoop and a cheer from behind and over to my left voices our guests' approval, and my mind flicks back to the hippie standing in the shadow of Cheddar. It seems as if that was all a long time ago, Captain Jaques and the dream of respectability.

Now is not the time to reminisce. It is my turn to go. What I couldn't sell at the circus I now give away again.

The barker, red-faced and jolly, cries out: 'Roll up, roll up. See the death-defiers in action! Gasp as they leap into the abyss.' But no. Nothing so theatrical. I step up on to the four-inch-wide parapet wall, a task which I doubt my ability to perform. Once standing there, balance is easy. It's amazing the confidence that having a parachute on gives you a few seconds after you've seen one work.

No wings beat. No sightless face turns toward me. Behind me the door gives on to a room of utter darkness. Nothing but the night hides there. Half smiling, I bend down, lean forward and at last, fully understanding, I surrender to the madness.

Epilogue

Excitement produces adrenaline, a chemical in the body
that raises one's metabolic rate, resulting sometimes in
exceptional performance. It is a direct link from the
psyche to the body. There is no doubt that people can
become addicted to adrenaline. The problem with addiction is widely thought to stem more from the addict's
personality than from the substance that is being abused.
Some people drink until they are drunk, but addicts drink
until it's all gone. The performance achieved while high
on adrenaline makes one feel good and other things start
to pale. Skydivers say that skydiving is life and everything
else is just waiting. Death is treated with bravado and
scorn. They wear T-shirts which read 'Cause of death –
IMPACT', and show funny cartoon characters seconds
from the bug-eyed staring monster called Groundrush.

But death really has no place on drop zones and only stops by there once in a while. There are hundreds of rules and restrictions which guard against death, and so the bravado is mostly false.

In ten years of skydiving from planes I have never met an experienced jumper who admits to being scared prior to exiting; indeed some say that the exit itself is the most joyous part of the jump. Conversely, after nine years in the company of BASE jumpers, I don't know of one who says he is not scared witless on the edge of a building or a cliff. This fear is well founded for, over the years, several people have died at various BASE jumping sites around the world. Even the founder of the BASE club, Carl Boenish, hit a cliff in Norway and lost his life. That's how terrible is the beauty to which we are drawn.

BASE is an acronym standing for Building, Antenna (radio or TV transmitter masts, like the one at Mendlesham), Spans (bridges), and Earth (cliffs). To qualify for a BASE number a person must jump successfully from each of these four fixed objects. Since the BASE club was started in 1981, only 320 people in the world have completed the circuit, though many more have jumped in one or two of these categories.

People were experimenting with 'parachutes' in ancient China and renaissance Europe long before the invention of aeroplanes, though the link between the two things was a natural one. The first person to die in a plane crash was its inventor, Orville Wright, and parachutes soon became a safety feature for pilots. The extra altitude that the development of flight made possible meant that parachuting in turn became safer. Today's parachute is as different from the original design as an F14 Tomcat from the

Wright brothers' wood frame and doped fabric biplane. Now, instead of descending straight down to a bone-jarring landing roll in army surplus boots, parachute landings are as soft as stepping from a kerbstone and jumpers often wear light sandals or go barefoot. Canopies are no longer round but rectangular and fly forward through the air with a glide angle far greater than their descent rate.

The technique of BASE jumping has also come a long way in the last ten years, though BASE jumpers and sky-divers still share laughter at one dictionary definition of base as 'a low and vulgar act'. With the modern canopy flying forward as well as down, a lot of research has been done to ensure that openings are 'on heading' – away from the structure. To those early daredevils, trial and error meant death or glory, until gradually they perfected the technique. Like the Wright brothers, who had a dream which others called crazy, they shared a camaraderie and a determination to make their dream come true. Now hundreds of BASE jumps are made each year without incident. Yet still I ask myself, each time I scale a rickety construction site fence at midnight, or slip inside some dusty tower block and prowl its booming corridors, 'Why am I here?' The answer comes not on any rooftop I have yet walked across.

I don't know what happened to my parachute on that dreadful night at the Barbican because the canopy was never retrieved and so I couldn't inspect it. Maybe a gust of wind arose at the moment of opening or a line snapped on one side of the chute; either would have caused the canopy to veer off as it did. Stunt men who calculate every detail on each stunt speak of 'variables', tiny 'what ifs' over which they have no control. BASE jumping certainly has its share of these, and we jump with this knowledge. Some BASE fatalities are caused by a parachute malfunction where the jumper impacts at very high speed with no canopy above him or her. More commonly deaths result from 'object strikes' similar to the one I experienced. In BASE jumping the variables tend to be unforgiving.

I'm writing this in California where a magazine is published called *The Fixed Object Journal* which disseminates information to BASE jumpers in the interests of furthering safety. Its editor, Nick Di Giovanni (BASE 194), told me when I asked why he BASE jumped, that he didn't know. Someone else helped him out with the usual 'Because it's fun,' while a third friend concluded that death was simply 'something that happens'. I learned that Nick keeps a file in which he records epitaphs or 'last words' from BASE jumpers, to be published in his magazine the morning after they scream into the tarmac. Typically Nick's own reads: 'I knew this would happen.' One week ago a much loved and respected BASE jumper died in Florida. He was driving from one drop zone to another late at night and hit a forty-ton truck head-on. He hadn't left anything in Nick's file but it's generally acknowledged that he would have agreed with the 'fun' angle.

This isn't as hard-hearted as it sounds because tears are also shed. There is a phone call late at night, a silence between friends at the drop zone, and then those of us left close ranks and carry on.

My companions in the story which you have just read were far more fortunate. After the first trip to the cliff

Steve never returned, and really I cannot blame him, for having had the experience myself I know how terrible those last few moments before impact can be. I saw him at Christmas three years ago, married and with a beautiful baby. We didn't talk about Cheddar for pleasure stamps memory more favourably than pain. Terry went on to make a few more leaps with a friend of his, they called themselves the 'Dangerous Brothers' but the pair were the only ones under any threat. I lost touch with Crazy Larry, and the last I heard of Kyle Ward he was learning to hang-glide. I hope the other pilots are ready for him. Dan Arlen had a major scare in the Gorge when he escaped a cliff strike by just a few inches. He was having second thoughts about whether to jump again and as I haven't seen him for two years now I don't know if he is really 'cured' or not.

Perhaps all of us have just grown a little older and so are more cautious now. But back then we were far more likely to shout at the devil than to whistle in the dark.

Simon Jakeman, BASE 60
California, 1992